For Jimmy —
a friend made at ...
and I hope to do it again
all the best
Oct 29 97

# ON PLANET EARTH

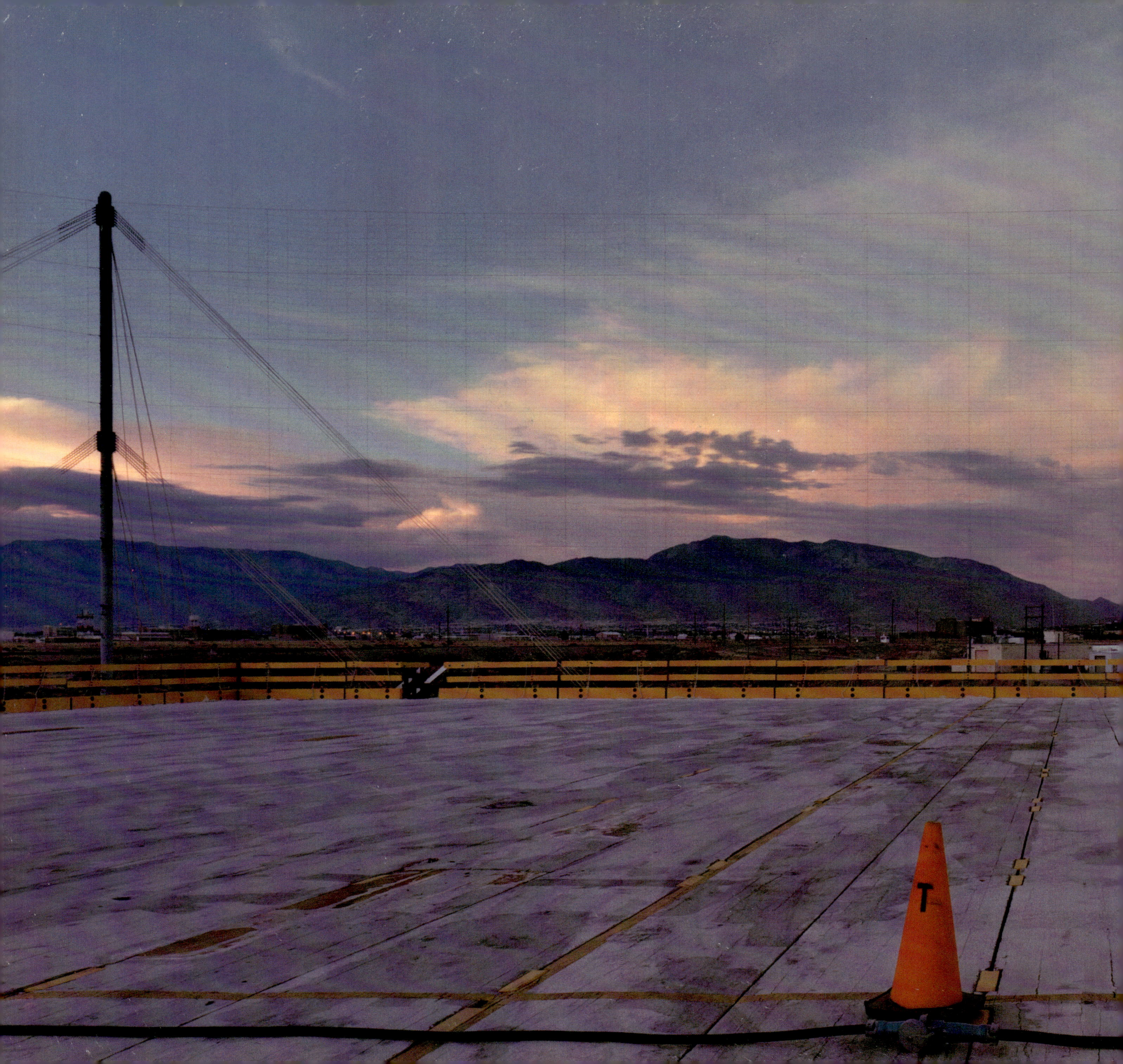
T

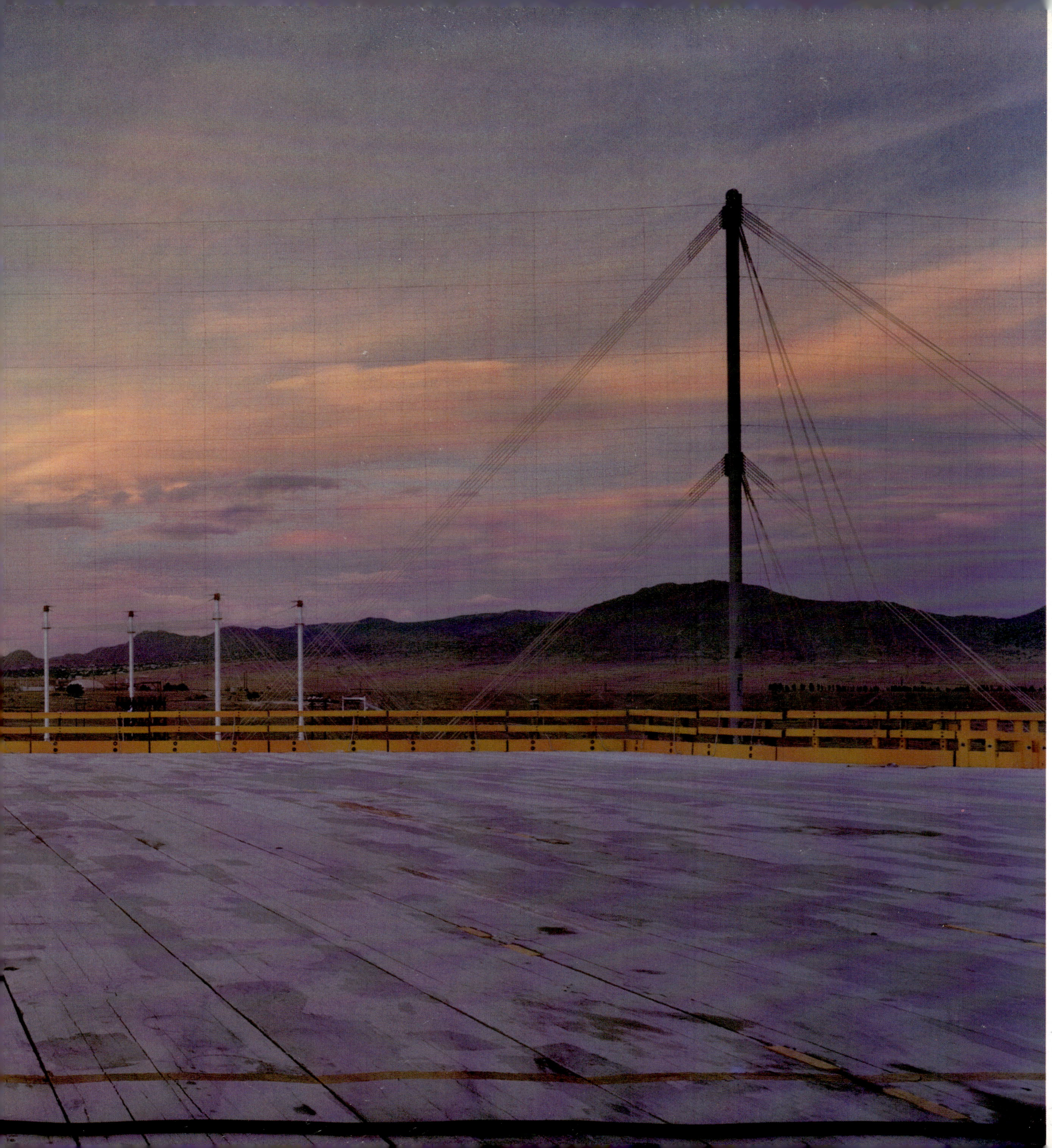

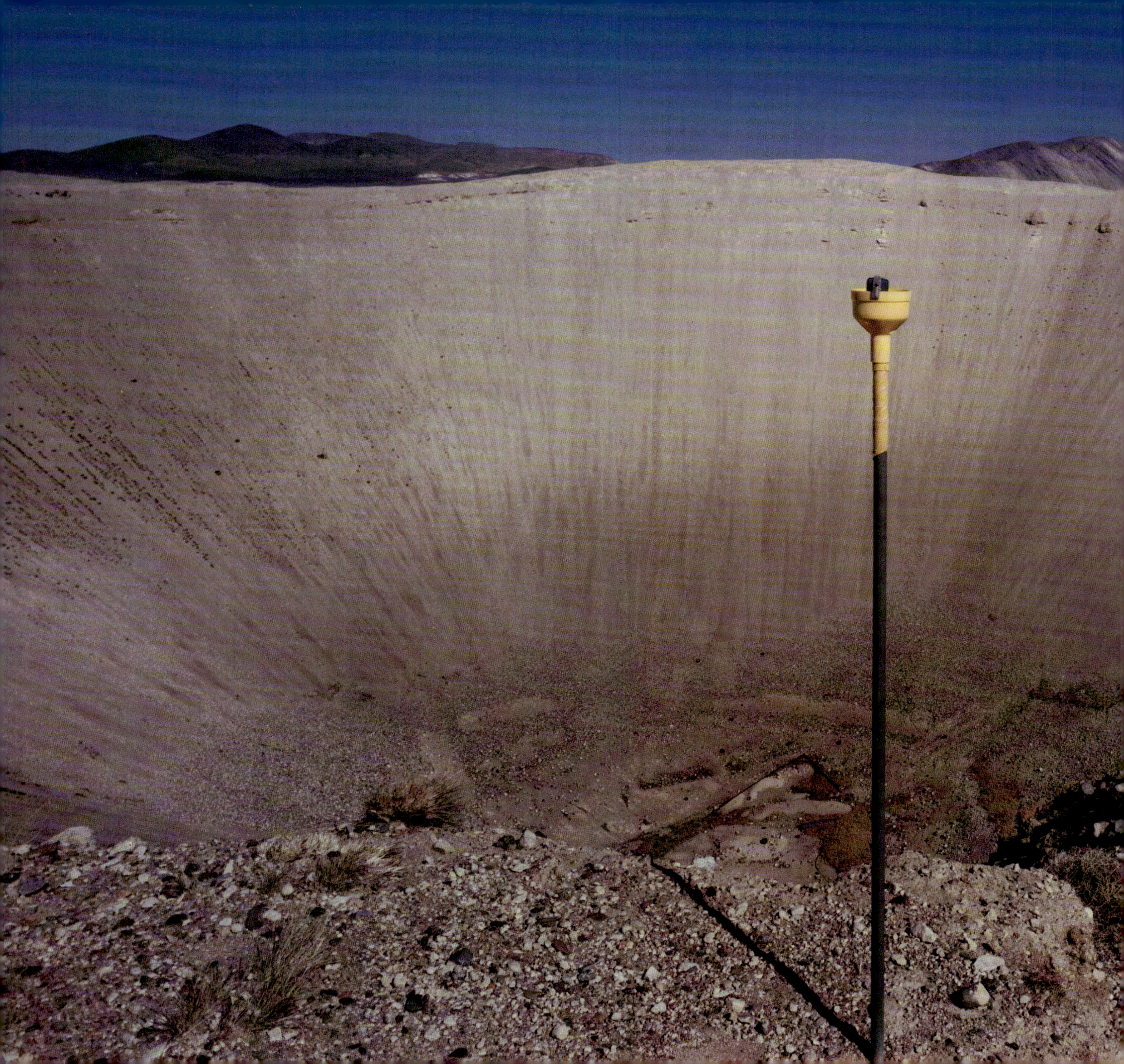

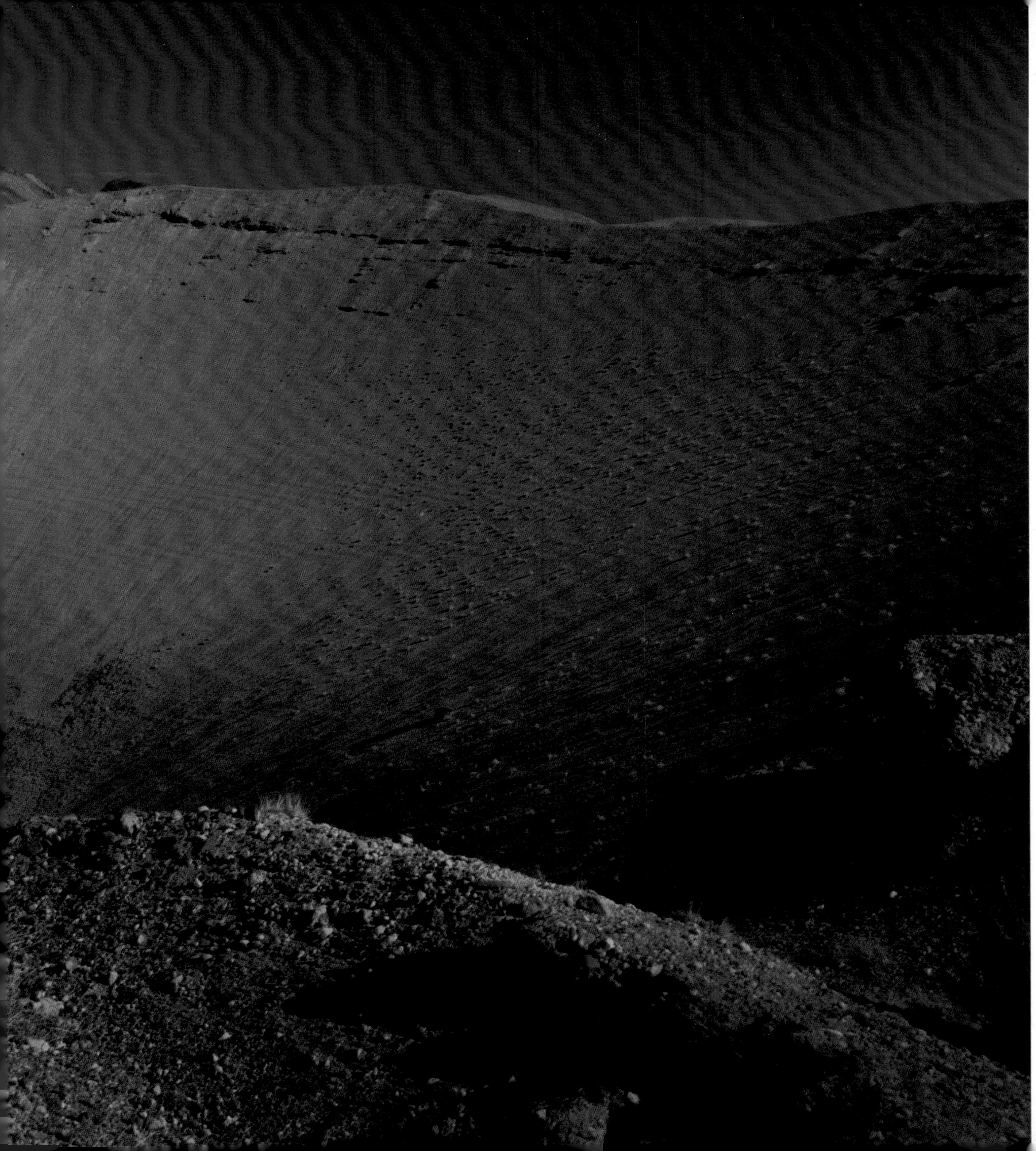

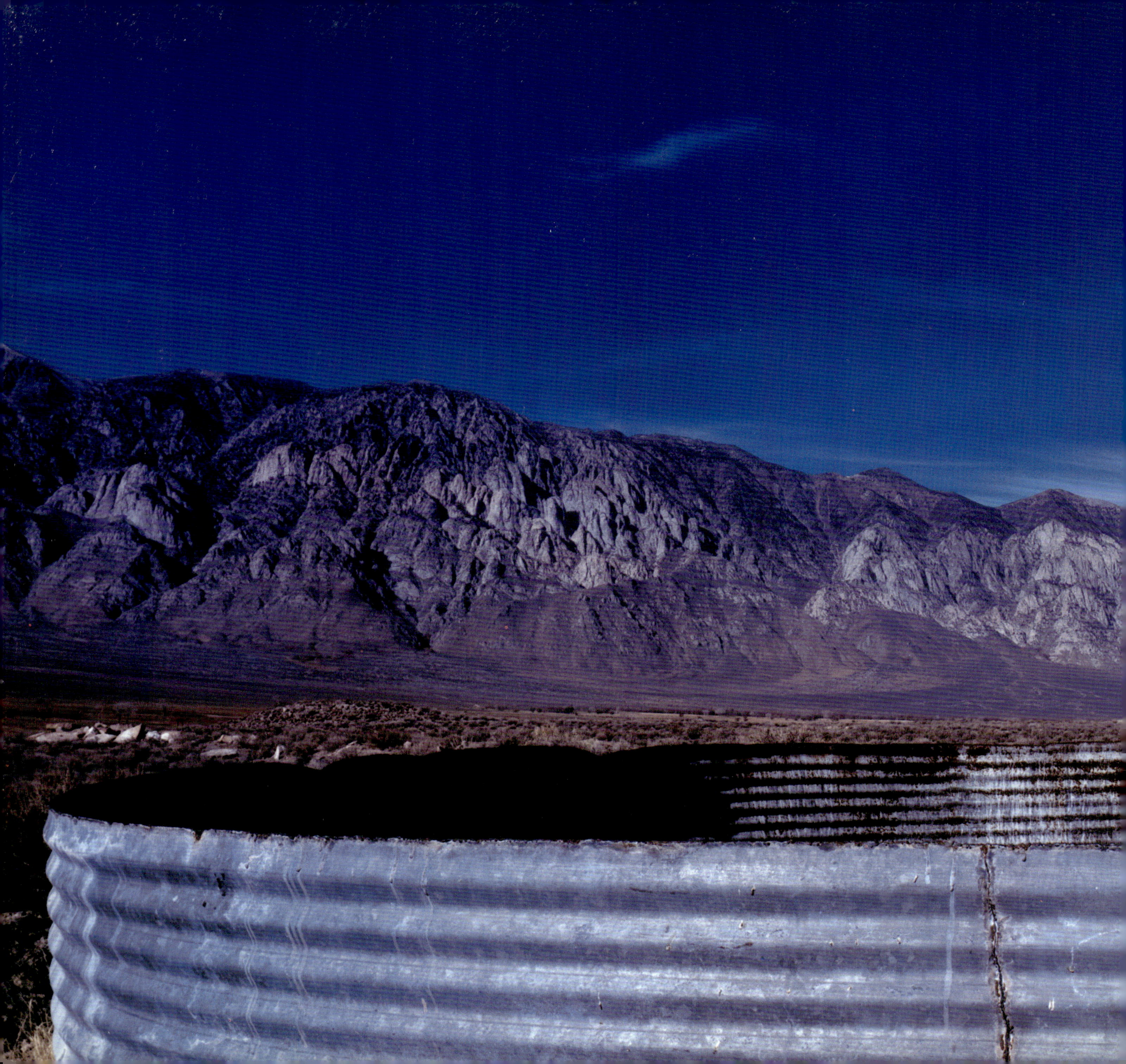

# ON PLANET EARTH

## TRAVELS IN AN UNFAMILIAR LAND

## PHOTOGRAPHS BY JAN STALLER

FLOOD PLAIN: An Original Story by LUC SANTE

APERTURE

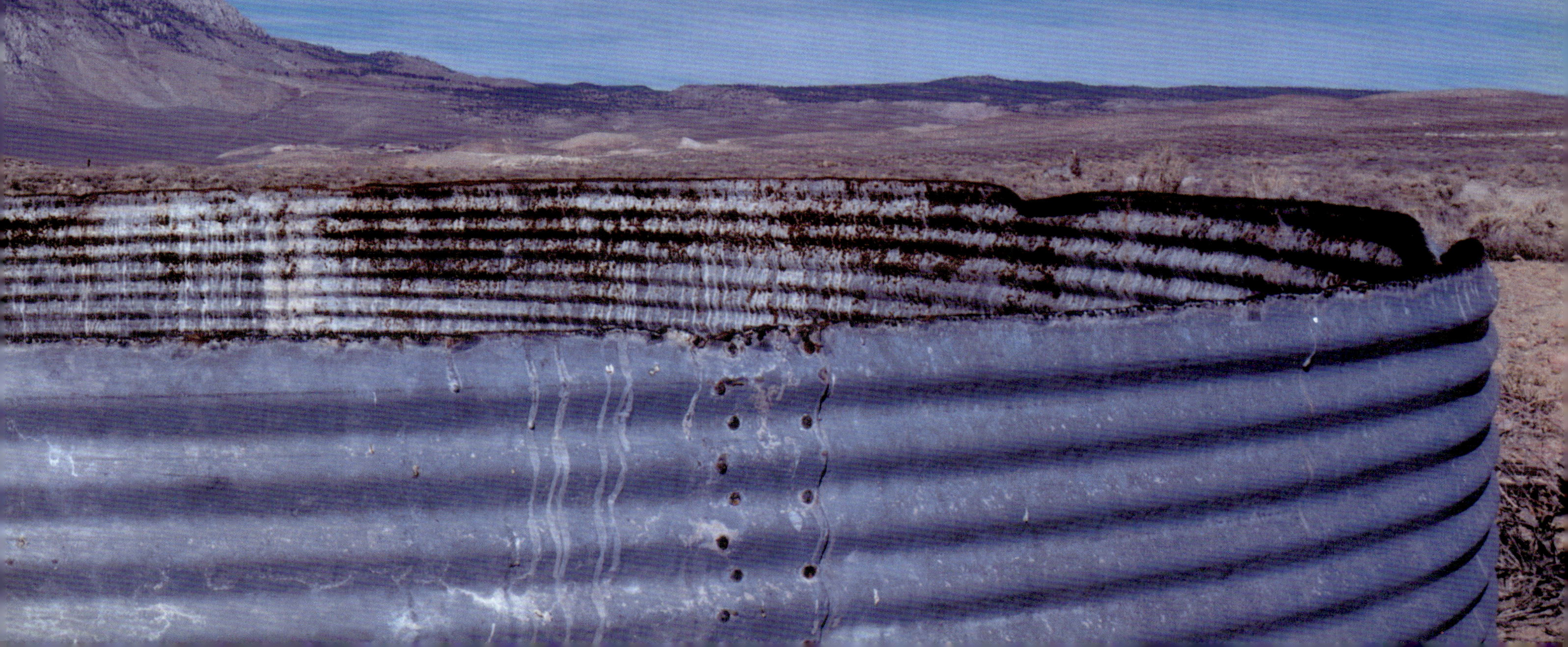

# FLOOD PLAIN

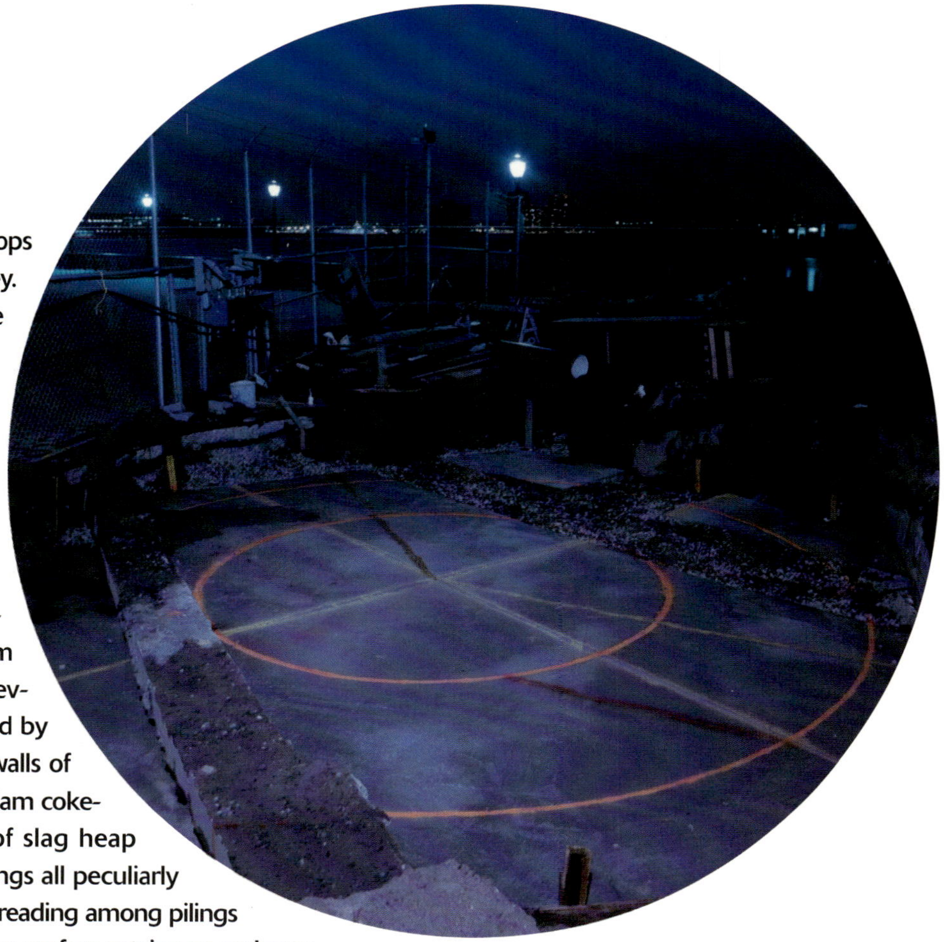

## BY LUC SANTE

**An hour past sunset,** party drops into affected zone, begins survey. Traveling around indeterminate body of former car located a dozen yards outside range of searchlight arcs, just beyond perimeter of unspecified and apparently vacant area delimited by hurricane fencing topped with concertina wire, to right of disused service road distinguished by buckled macadam pocked with weed-sprouted crevices, along artificial ridge formed by buried remains of foundation walls of number three building of quondam coke-smelting plant, skirting base of slag heap grown over with ailanthus saplings all peculiarly bent rightward at their stems, threading among pilings of partly-collapsed billboard whose surface retains several numbers and scattering of letters and blurred image of nose-cone mated with cigarette filter, over dorsal growth banked with gravel and furrowed with ghost impressions of rail ties, helter-skelter through irregular patch of salt marsh festooned with doorless refrigerators and lidless washing machines reposing at unnatural angles, halting temporarily at unsecured lot containing remains of apparent experiment involving sundry disproportionate orange plastic plinths and quantity of braided steel cable.

**At midnight**, texture and grade of ground surface barely guessable between passes of searchlight arcs and then utterly obscure outside their range, sky overhead an opaque clay red, every compass point of horizon aglow with gaseous aura transmitted upward by what might be dozens of simultaneous chemical-plant explosions whose collective boom is so intense as to be (paradoxically) equivalent to loaded silence, actually drowned out by continuous F-sharp vibrational hum produced by traffic streaming over half-rotted girders of ancient suspended roadway five miles south. Tremor of uncertain origin pulses intermittently underfoot, causing instrument needles to flicker wildly and light grids to blink on and off in erratic sequences. Eighty-six degrees Fahrenheit, 90 percent humidity, wind from the east, sulfurous with hint of brine, elevated ozone levels. Swamp gas, ignis fatuus, methane flashes, etc. The occasional formless, odorless, noiseless, invisible *presence*. Pulse rate abnormal. Breathing strained.

**False dawn**. Now proceeding northwest through area of yellow-green sucking mud, phosphorescent on contact. Geiger counter clicks, clicks again, chirrups. One member of party (cryptobotanist) unaccounted for. Map coordinates apparently indicate area to be former site

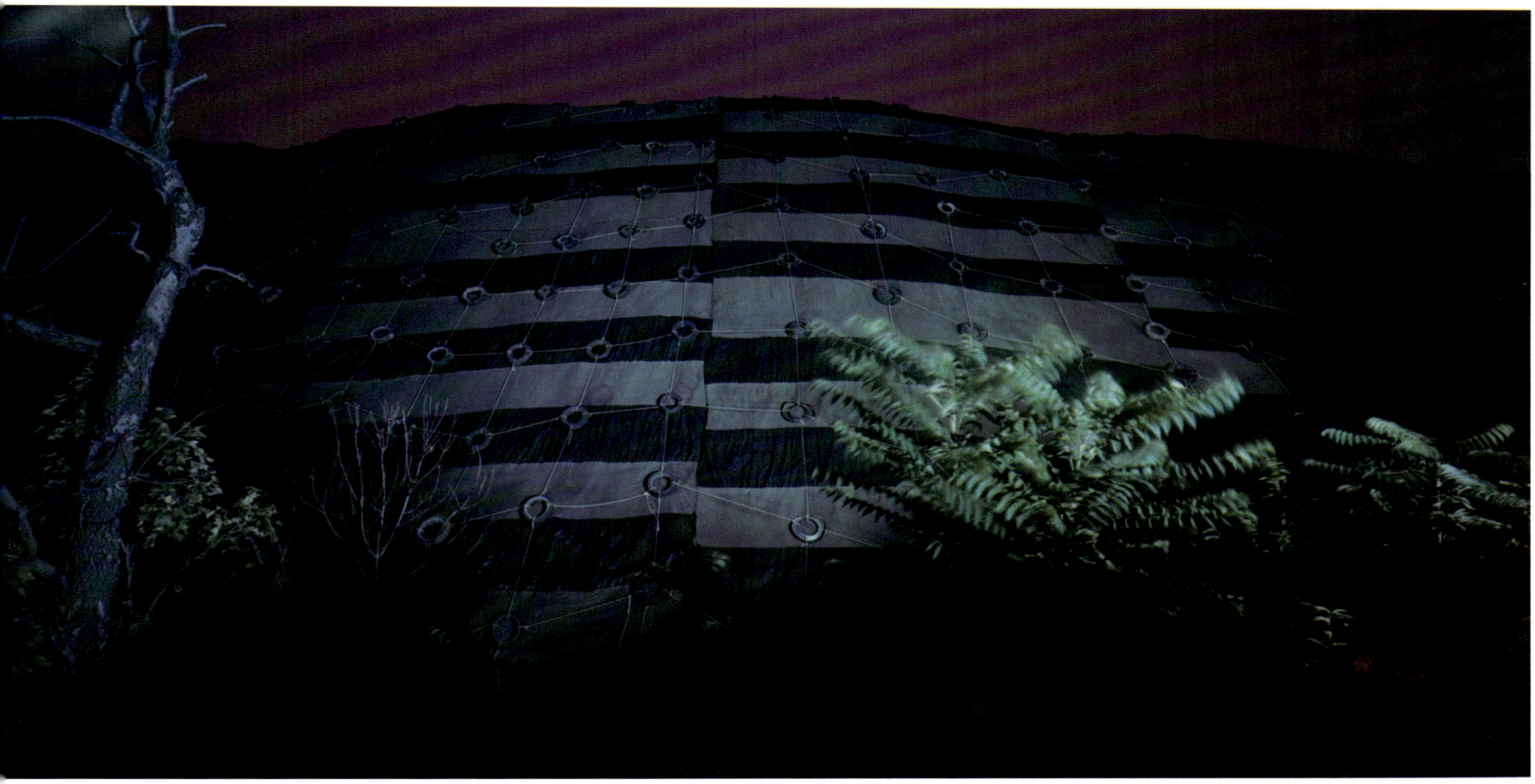

of multistory car park adjacent to sports arena complex, although this seems unlikely. Coordinates possibly miscalculated. Patches of extreme temperature fluctuation, perhaps caused by subterranean chemical lakes or maybe prolonged bituminous combustion, but attempts at excavation only result in loss of tools. Vegetation resumes, albeit of dubious origin, along with gradual increase in solidity of ground surface. Here and there concrete remnants resembling stumps, scattered asphalt islets that become more frequent until they take on semblance of road, leading to large level terrain with more-or-less rectilinear boundaries. Party (now three unaccounted for) establishes campsite.

**First light**. Shallow search of immediate area begins, with goal of determining preliminary single-epoch cultural profile. Inventory: chrome hubcaps in diverse styles, pottery fragments, kitchen-midden deposits (shinbones, glass shards, razor-clam shells, humanoid teeth), empty beer cans ranging from steel construction with visible seam and triangular perforation effected with hand tools to molded aluminum with die-cut droplet-shaped hole or ovoid hole with attached metal ring, flint and granite spearheads, skull with bowl-shaped depression in crown, flexible watch strap, transparent plastic bags, radiator hose, ox mandible. Salt-encrusted length of bicycle chain, nylon sheeting, whetstone, amulets, maize-grinding apparatus, polyvinyl chloride siphon tube, substantial array of printed paper bits. Seventy-three truck and 228 automobile tires, horseshoe-crab carapaces, onyx knife, very large titanium-alloy disk with hatchway unyielding to crowbar. Collected material herded under tarpaulin after logging and tagging.

**Mid-morning**. Party (now missing four members) continuing northwest under highway overpass. Traffic moderate to heavy with minor rubbernecking delays due to stalled tractor-trailer in passing lane. Low cloud cover, maximum humidity, no precipitation. Billboards advertise tropical resorts, beer, automobiles, assorted gizmos. Terrain abruptly falls away, descent effected with rappelling rig improvised from perimeter-marking cord. Yellow-ochre haze blows in from the east, making progress slow at first, hazardous at length, eventually immobilizing group on defunct highway-access ramp within impenetrable cloud. Remaining members, although fully suited and equipped with oxygen

apparatus, experience difficulty breathing, become subject to variably vivid hallucinations, report disturbing emergence of repressed childhood memories. Fights break out (effectiveness of blows impeded by suiting); one member runs amok wielding corroded exhaust pipe found at site (eventually overwhelmed and subdued by others); one member suffers grand mal seizure (impossibility of depressing tongue without opening face-shield causes concern, but trauma passes without inflicting permanent damage); one member tears off suit and runs south, naked and gagging, collapses a hundred yards away, coughs twice and expires (corpse wrapped in parachute and prepared for portage to feasible burial location). Finally calm restored as remnants of party sit silently and await directional change of wind.

**Noon**. Under blazing sun, party wends through automobile graveyard, pausing to inter deceased forensic anthropologist in vault formed by vacant exoskeletons of two matched lime-green Ford Fiestas. Core samples taken of flattened ex-vehicles reposing in fifteen-foot stacks. Theoretical foundation for preliminary taxonomy of hood ornaments debated in brief session. Recently extinguished cooking fire found at mouth of white Dodge Caravan carcass. Examination of interior reveals foam-rubber bedding, stray clothing elements, professional wrestling

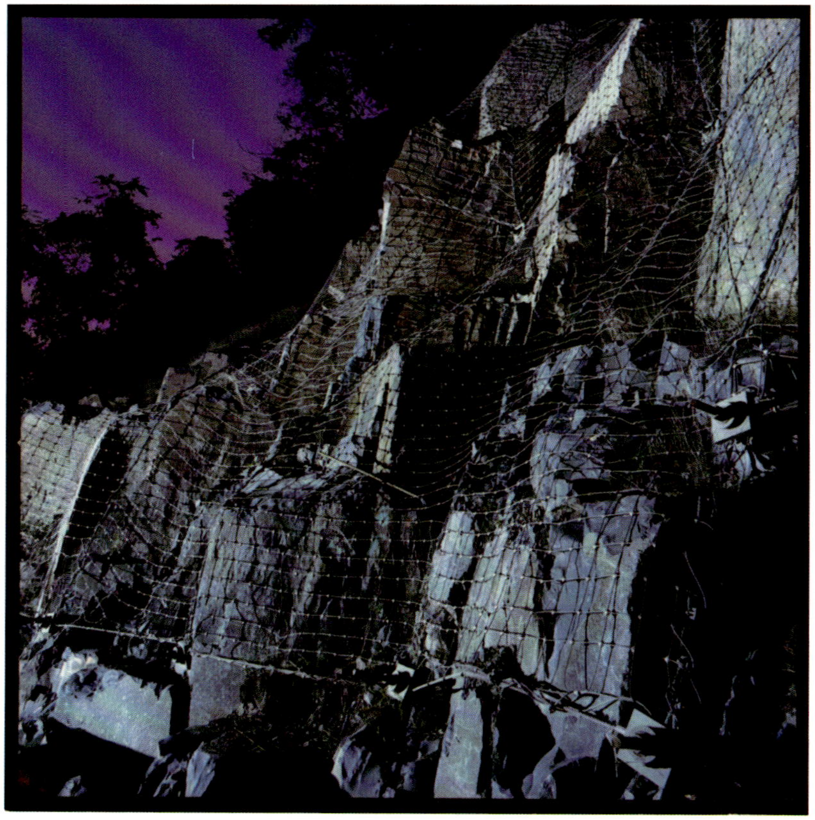

magazines, unopened tins of Vienna sausage, partly fossilized pizza crusts, ritual altar, jar containing goat umbilicus. Decision to leave site undisturbed immediately breached by member found looting. Member handcuffed but permitted to continue expedition otherwise unmolested. Party circumnavigates mattress outlet, big and tall men's clothing warehouse, factory-closeout shoe mart, and several evidently competing dinette purveyors. Members dissimulate themselves in underbrush and observe actions of clientele parking vehicles, entering, and leaving sometimes bearing packages. Particular interest taken regarding slipshod means of attaching bulky items to vehicle roofs using twine. Temperature

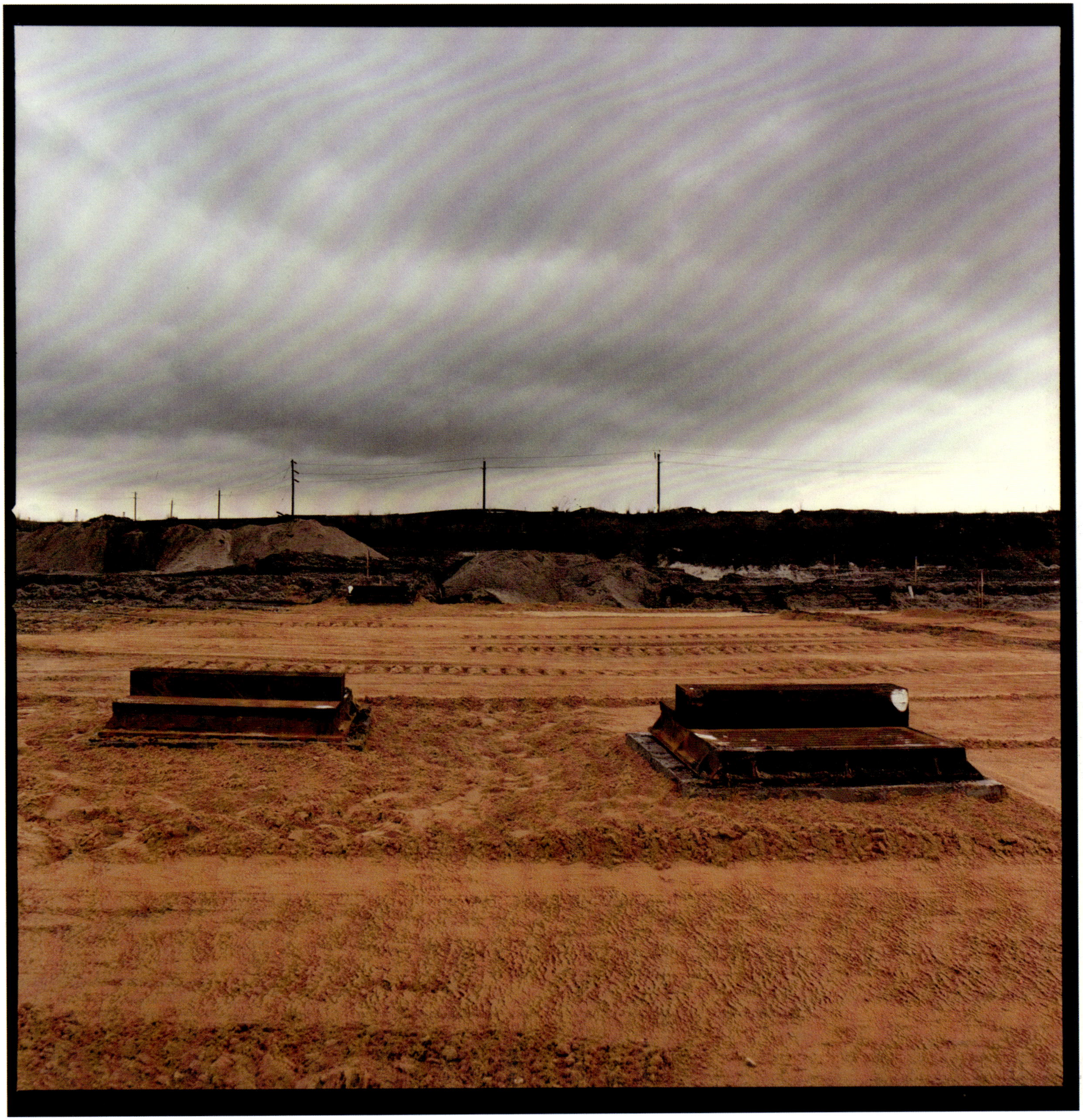

over 100° Fahrenheit, air quality poor, terrain spongy with extensive growth of fluorescent moss. Three members report apparently simultaneous visions of gigantic glowing ambulatory figure to the west, but disagree as to whether its nature could best be described as humanoid or reptilian.

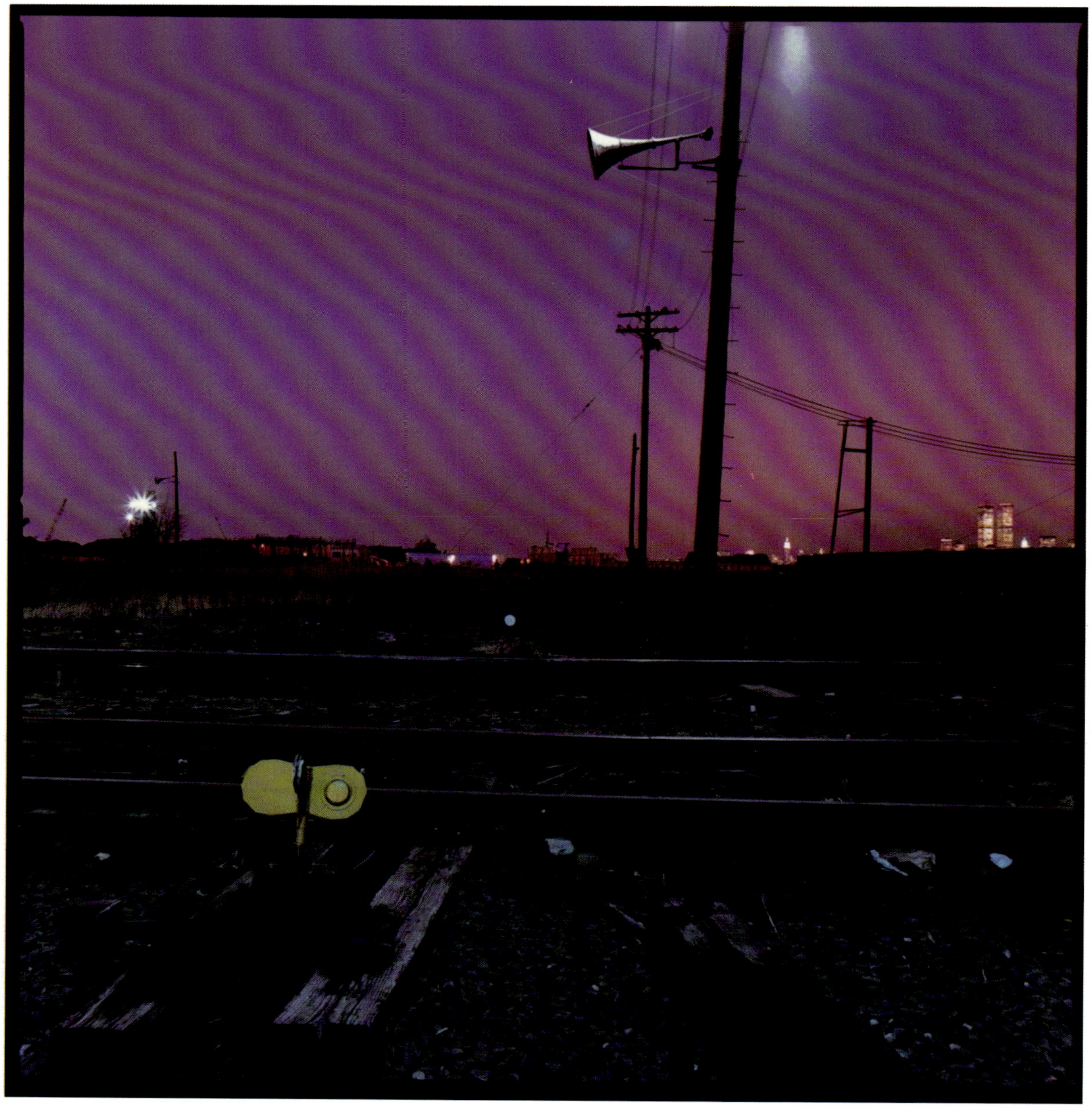

**Post-meridian** finds party entering salt marsh of unknown depth, electing to link themselves together at their waists using spliced length of perimeter-marking cord. This proves wise even while cumbersome, as submerged objects continually impede progress. One member's foot caught and nearly mashed by what turns out to be side panel of air-conditioning unit, another's suit torn by jagged corner of blasted Diebold safe (tear hastily mended with criss-cross patch of duct tape). On far shore, as members unknot themselves, end of cord found shorn and blackened—only sign of loss of tectonic geologist in caboose position. Party now halved by six. Morale correspondingly low. Attention diverted in time by appearance of vast tract of dead-storage warehouses, many seemingly long unvisited. One such building chosen at random is measured and searched for possible means of ingress. As others hastily ingest nutritional bars, engineer saws through padlocks on side door. Inside, probe lights frustratingly ineffectual in cutting through suspended mist of dust particles, members hurtle about stubbing toes and bruising flanks on randomly disposed large wooden crates. Decision reached to investigate contents of one standing alone, bound with iron straps. Prised open, it emits, first, deep roaring sound, and then what is described as intense white light, blinding three members nearest to it. Entire party rushes from warehouse in panic. Outside, sightless meteorologist, applied phenomenologist, theoretical linguist continue running.

**Just before sunset.** Beleaguered remaining three members ascertain coordinates, begin trek back to drop zone. Progress slow through area of unaccountably outsized lichen, bluish-gray and waving faintly in sluggish breeze. Commuter traffic backed up for miles due to chemical spill near freeway interchange. Blimp advertising distilled-spirits manufacturer passes overhead. Handcuffed epidemiologist suddenly

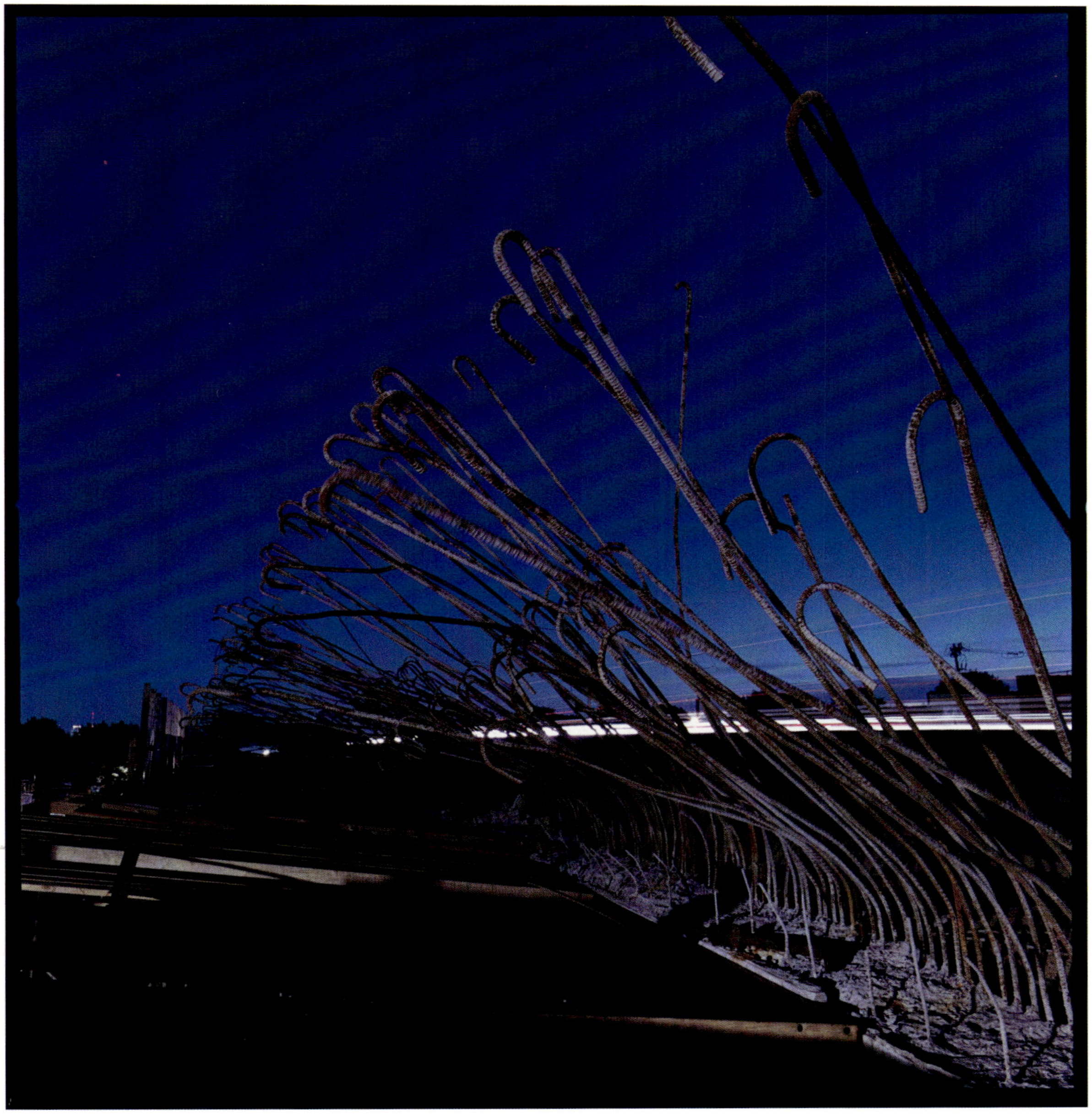

bolts onto highway during momentary forward spurt of vehicles in rightmost lane, run over by bakery truck. Sun now appears as sickly melting orange coughdrop, languidly spreading over western horizon. Gulls circle cawing, dropping deformed mussel shells on concrete pilings of unbuilt overpass. Two survivors wander through field of earth augers. One of three blinded members observed staggering, occasionally falling, at distance across phantom overpass, but identity cannot be established owing to anonymous inflated yellow protective suiting. Survivors, at apparent cul-de-sac formed by angles of three roadways, argue over direction of drop zone as compass needle gyrates wildly. Roadways appear to shift, rise, fall. Angry shouts transmitted as unintelligible pink noise by speaker units in face shields. Paleochemist produces entrenching tool, engineer two-foot drill bit, flail at each other, rending suit materials, which tatter in long strands, but lack strength to inflict actual bodily injury. Actions increasingly clumsy, both stumble, collapse.

**Midnight**. Engineer finds self on hands and knees, crawling through electrical substation. No sign of other. Pauses to observe mating patterns of ball lightning atop dynamo units. Mesmerized by intricate courtship dance of yellow-white energy spheroids coquettishly separating and rejoining along power cables. Slowly realizes blackness of sky, lack of electric lighting anywhere in field of vision. Crawls through indistinct terrain strewn with thorny underbrush, vaguely conscious of cuts, momentarily cooling spurts of blood. Imagines self carving holiday turkey, family gathered in candlelit room, children gurgling, cackling, poultry carcass oddly expanding to fill room. Prolonged unconsciousness. Sees helicopter hovering, ladder descending, but cannot reach same, cannot verify material reality or lack thereof. Desperation becomes panic, involuntary arm movements. Collides with and then clutches object: shopping cart. Stands. Pushes cart down aisle: stationery, misses and juniors, hardware, automotive, patio furniture. Aisle succeeds aisle. Mood increasingly cheerful, recognizes catchy ambient tune. Prices attractive, discounts substantial, tempting. Attempts to recall shopping list.

*Dedicated to my parents in recognition of the many inspirations and support that they have provided for my work.*

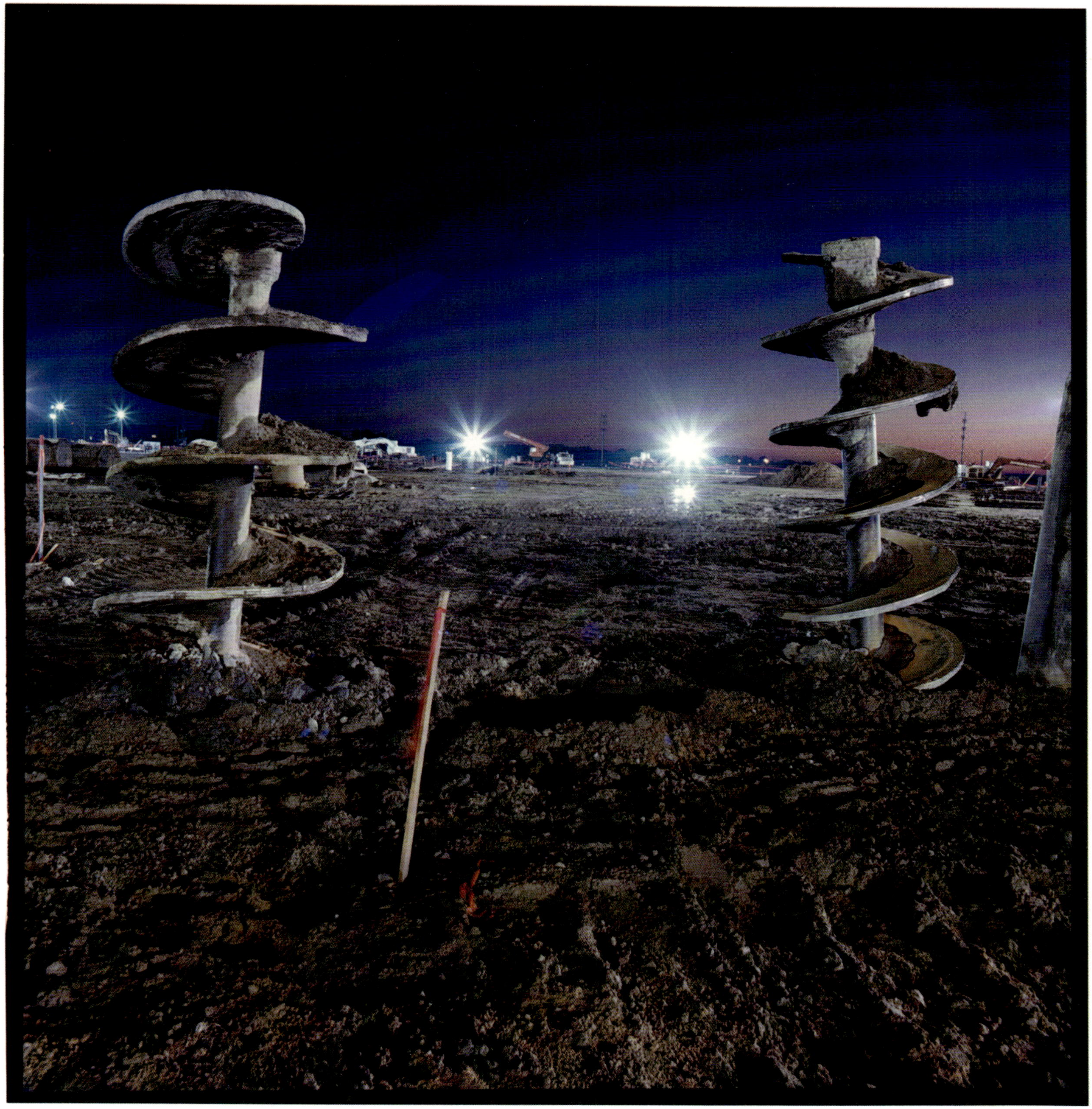

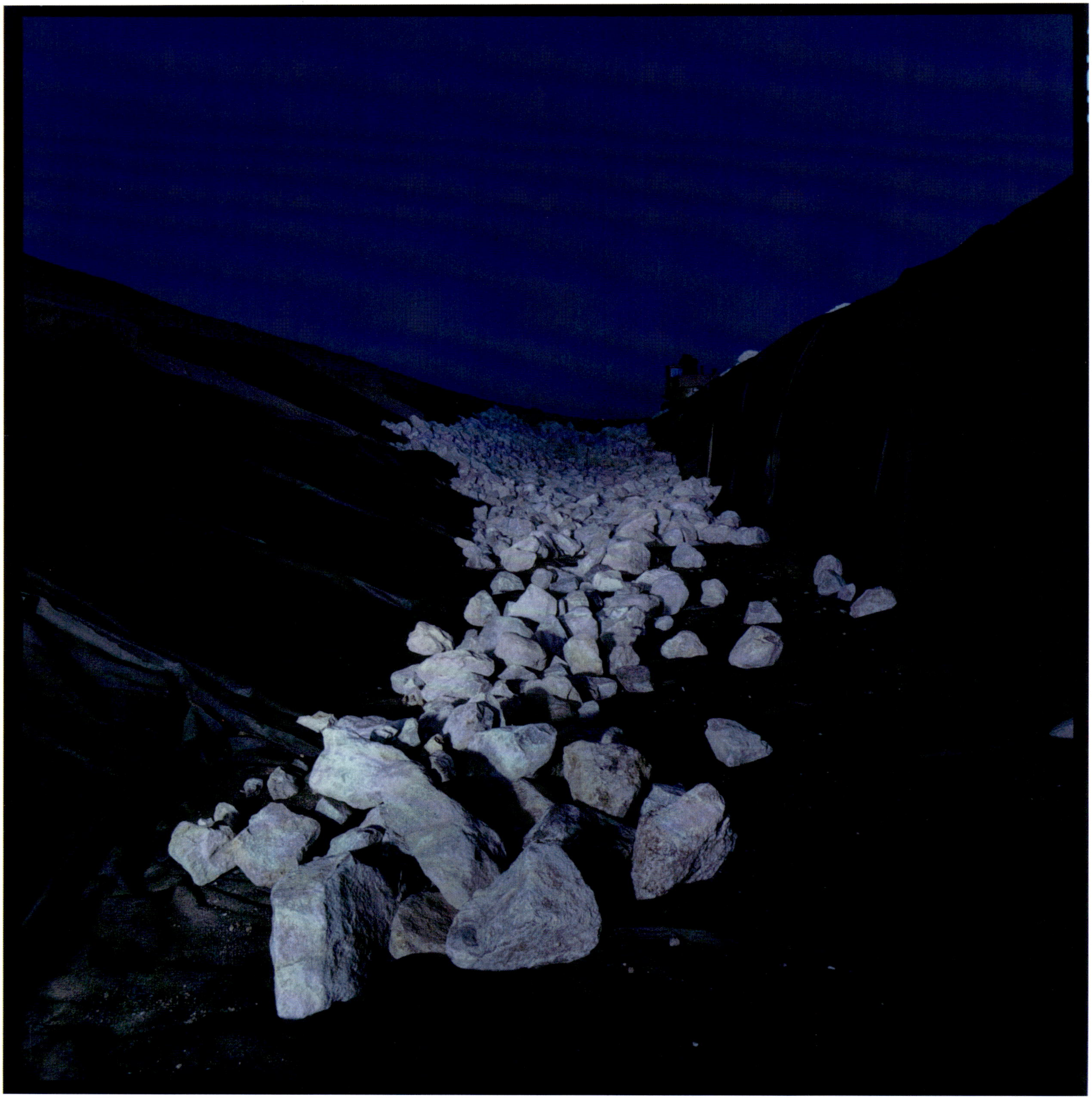

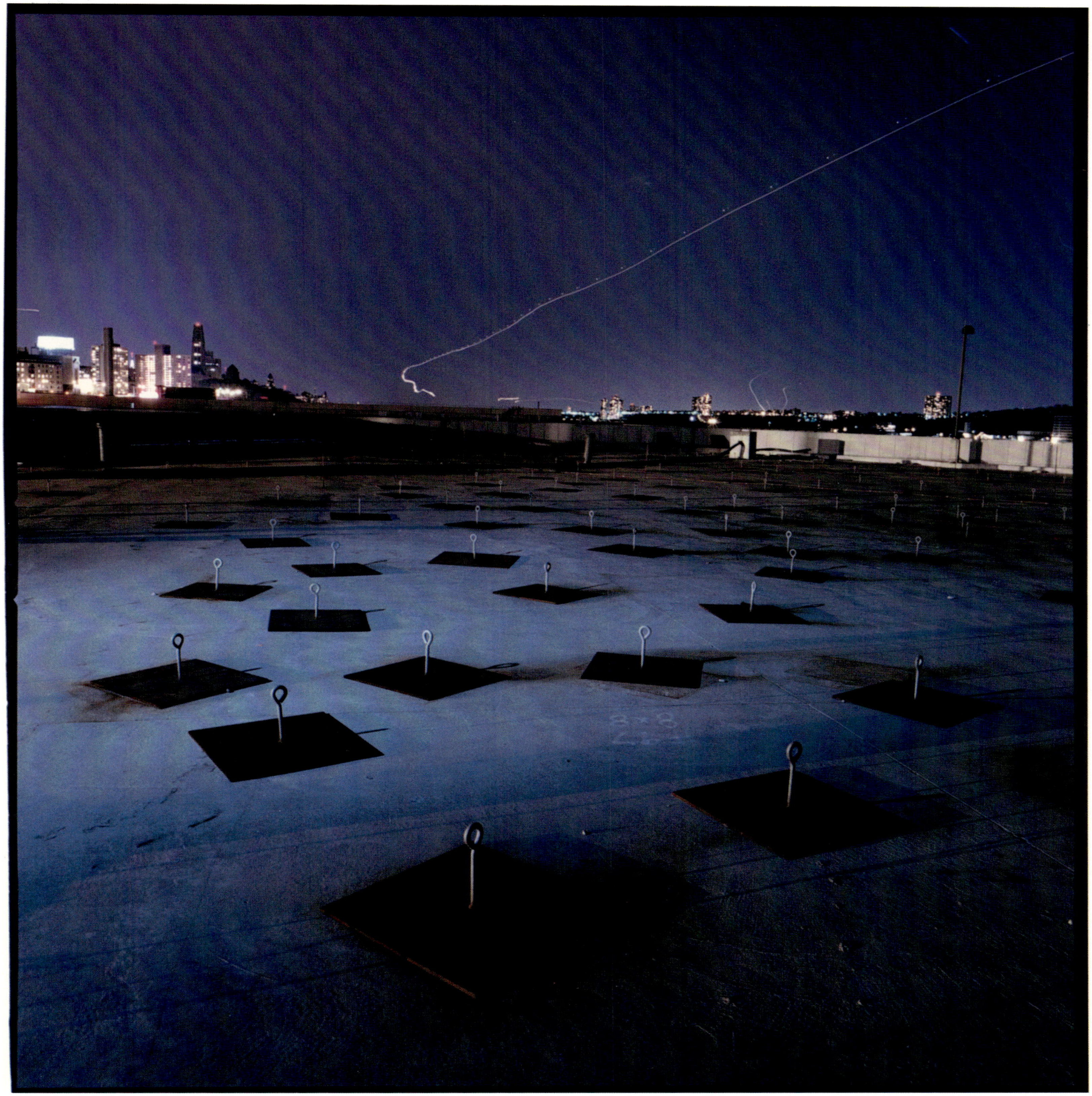

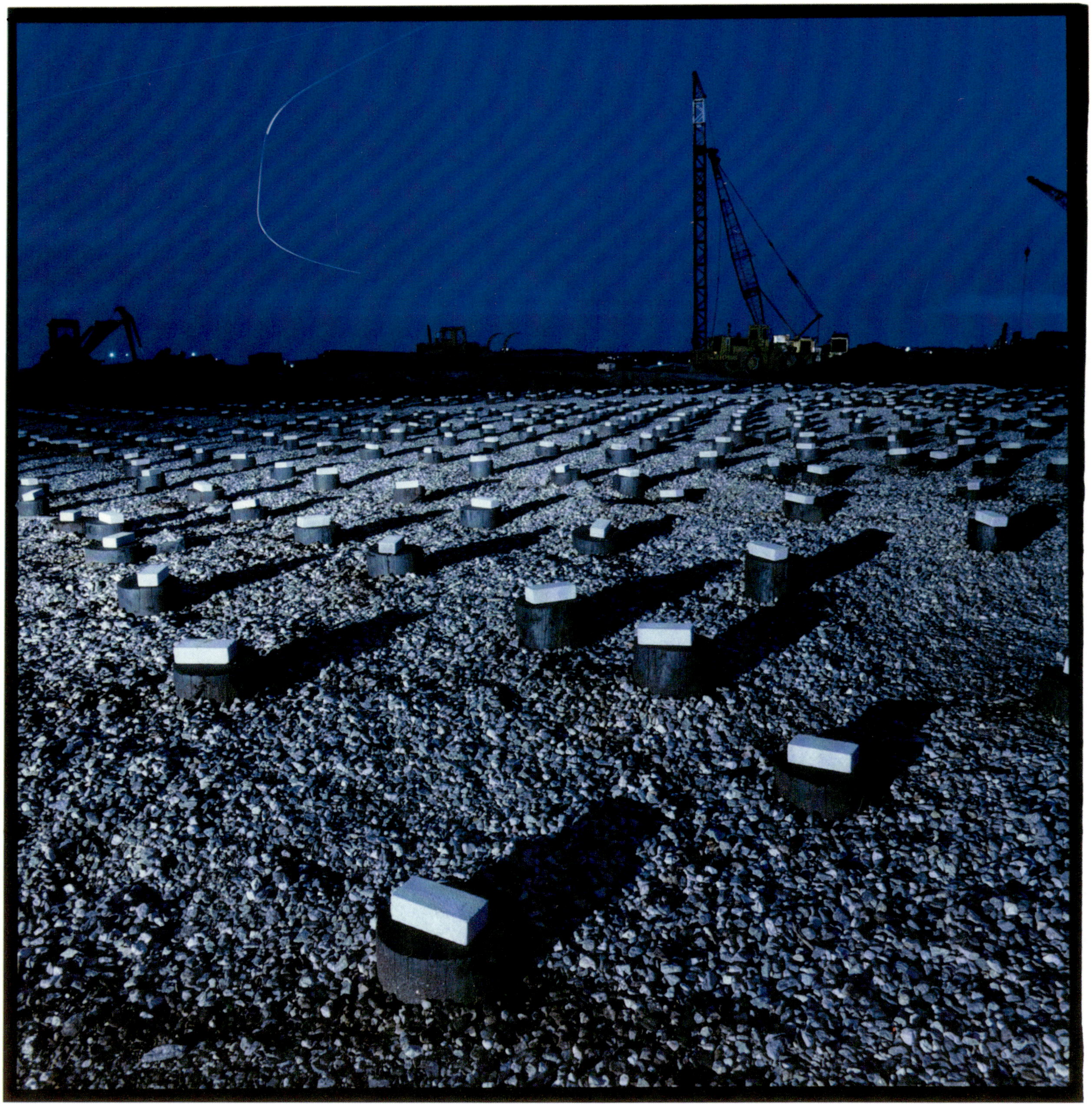

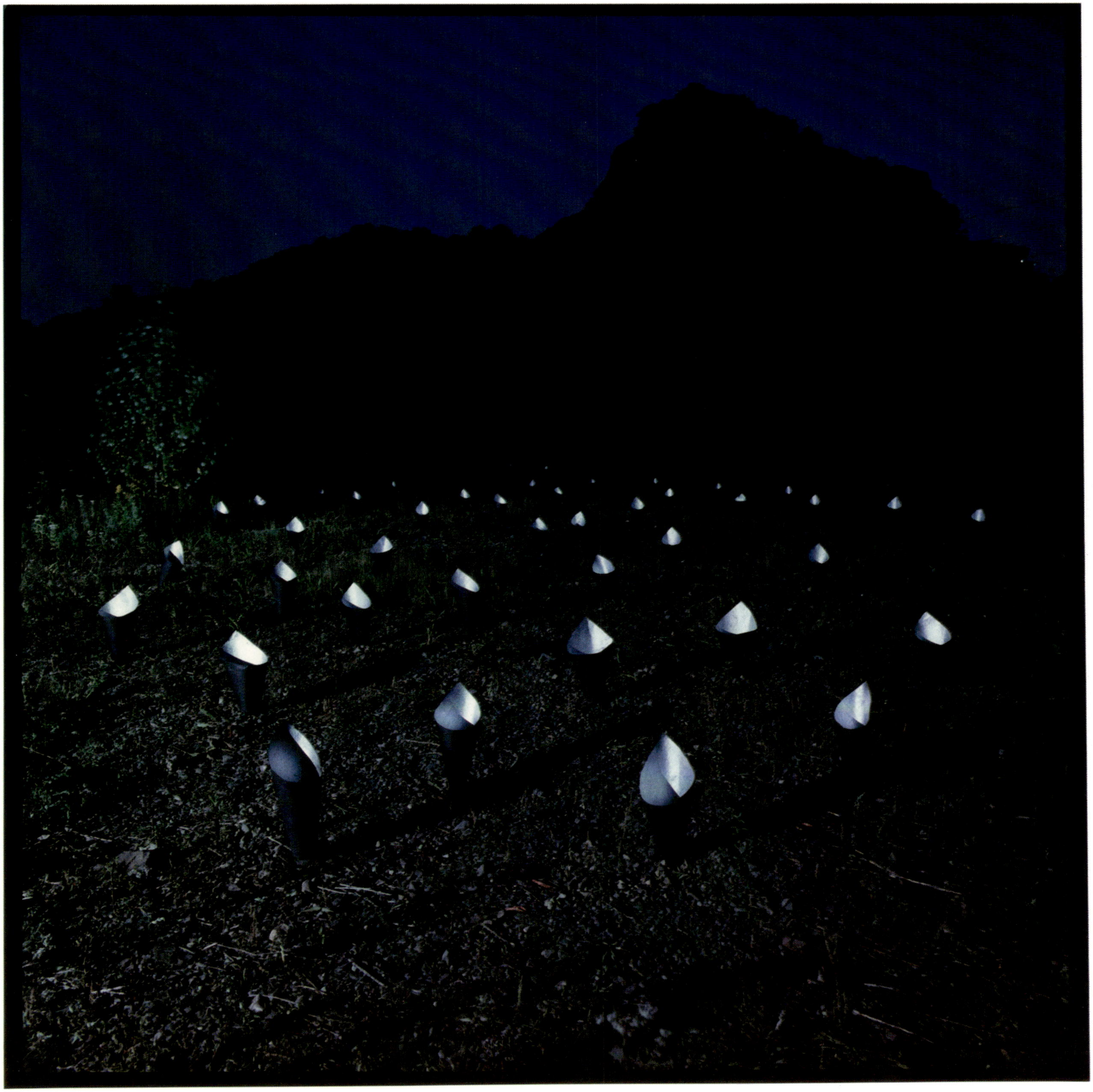

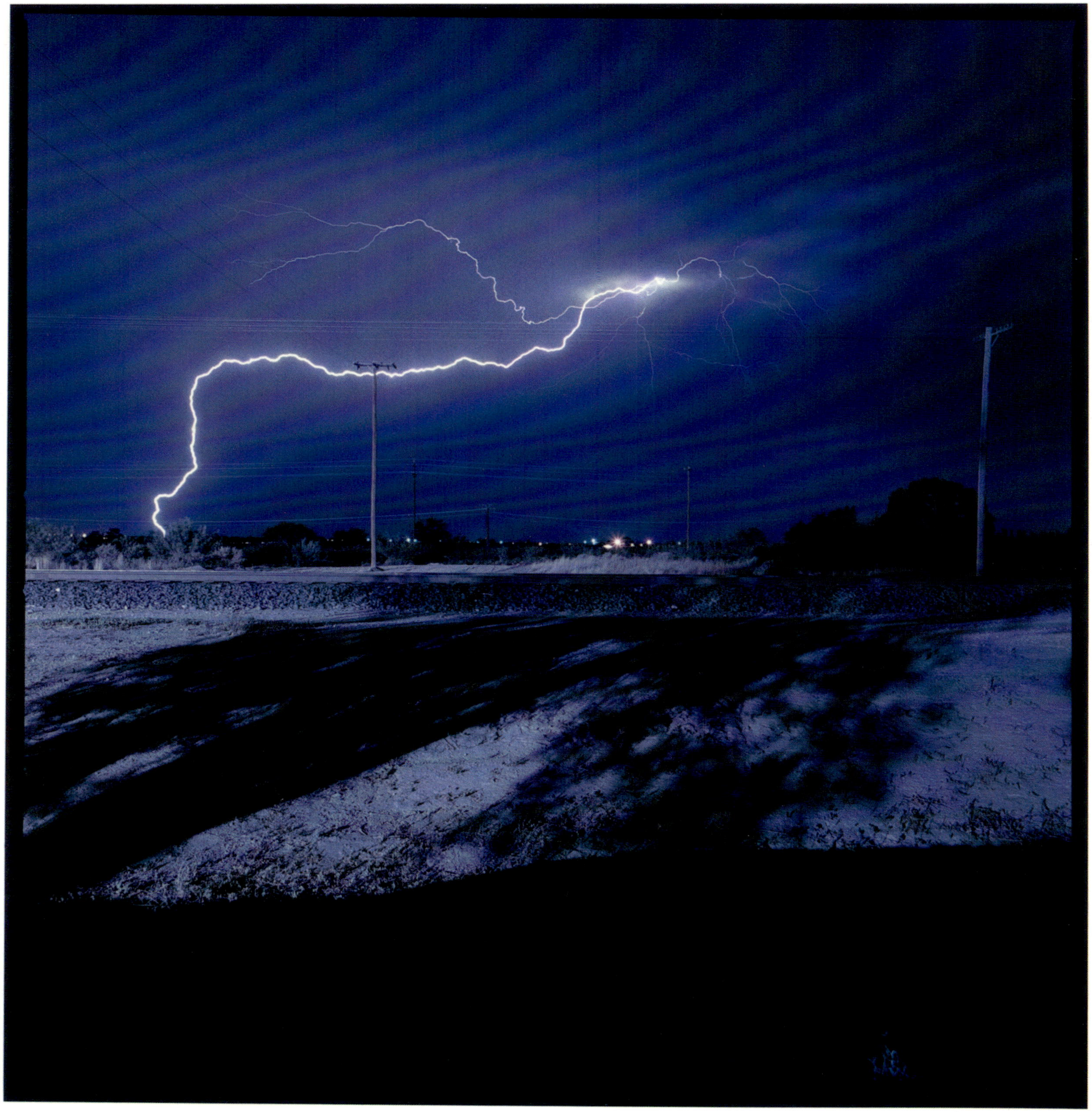

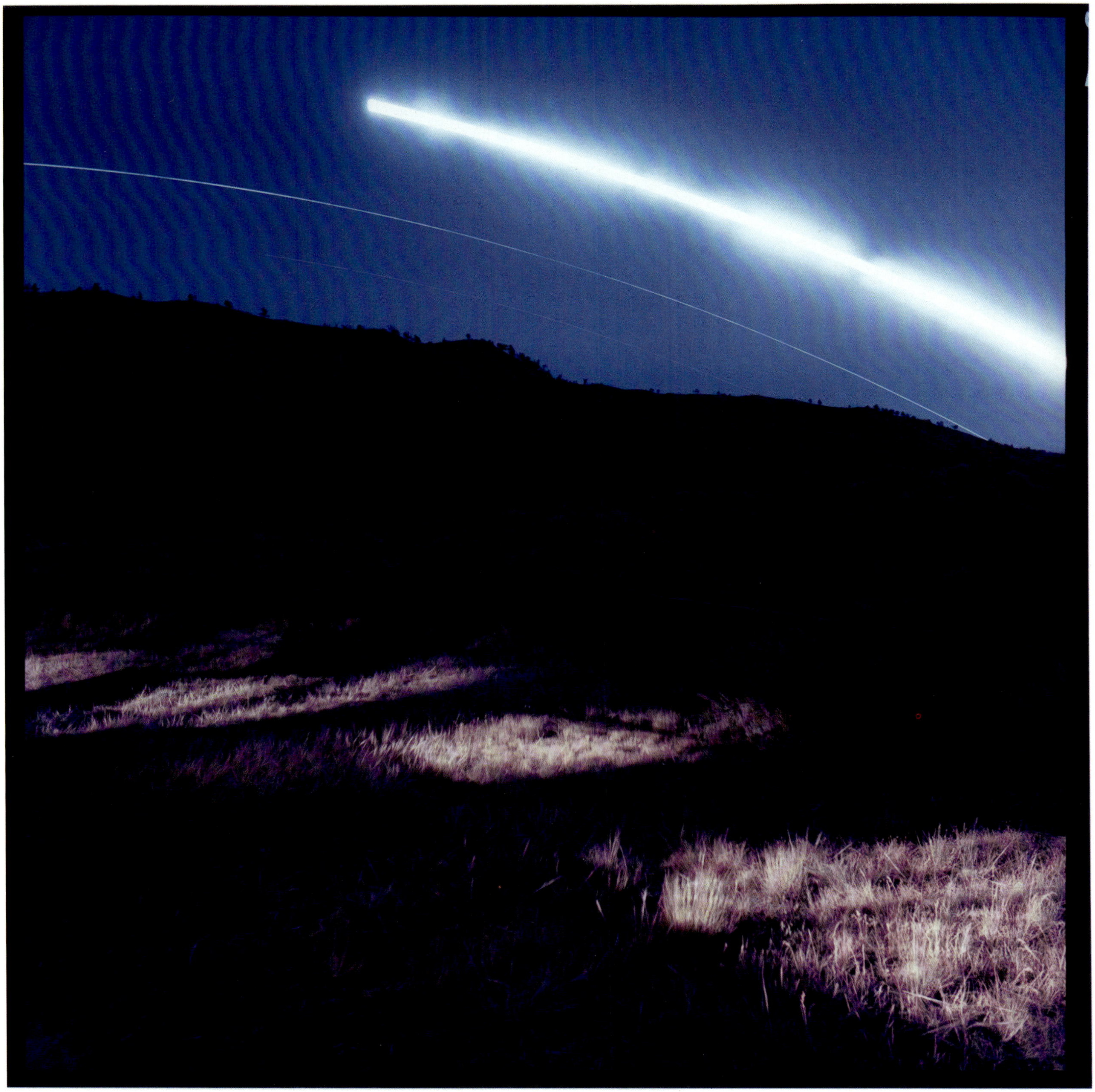

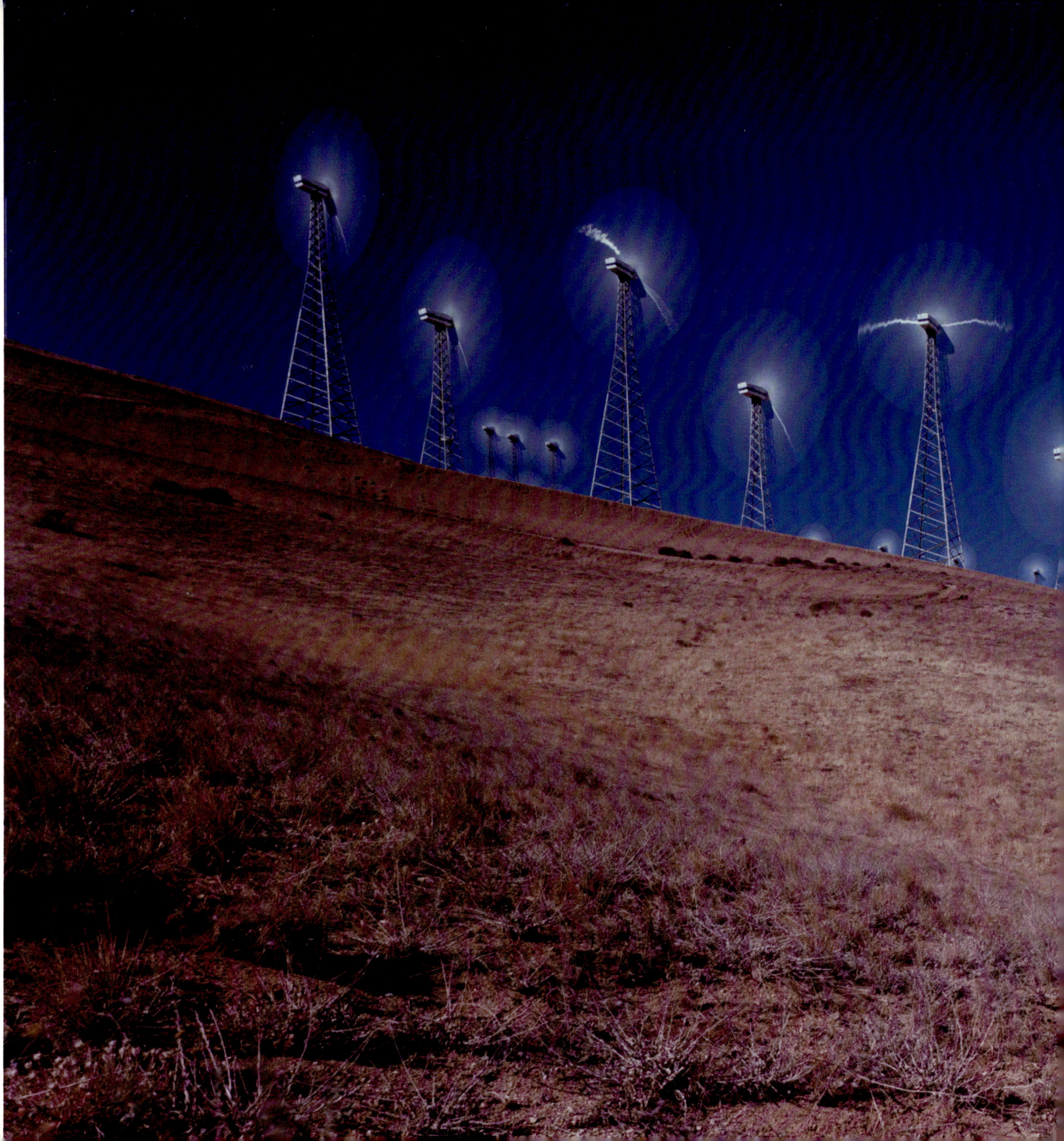

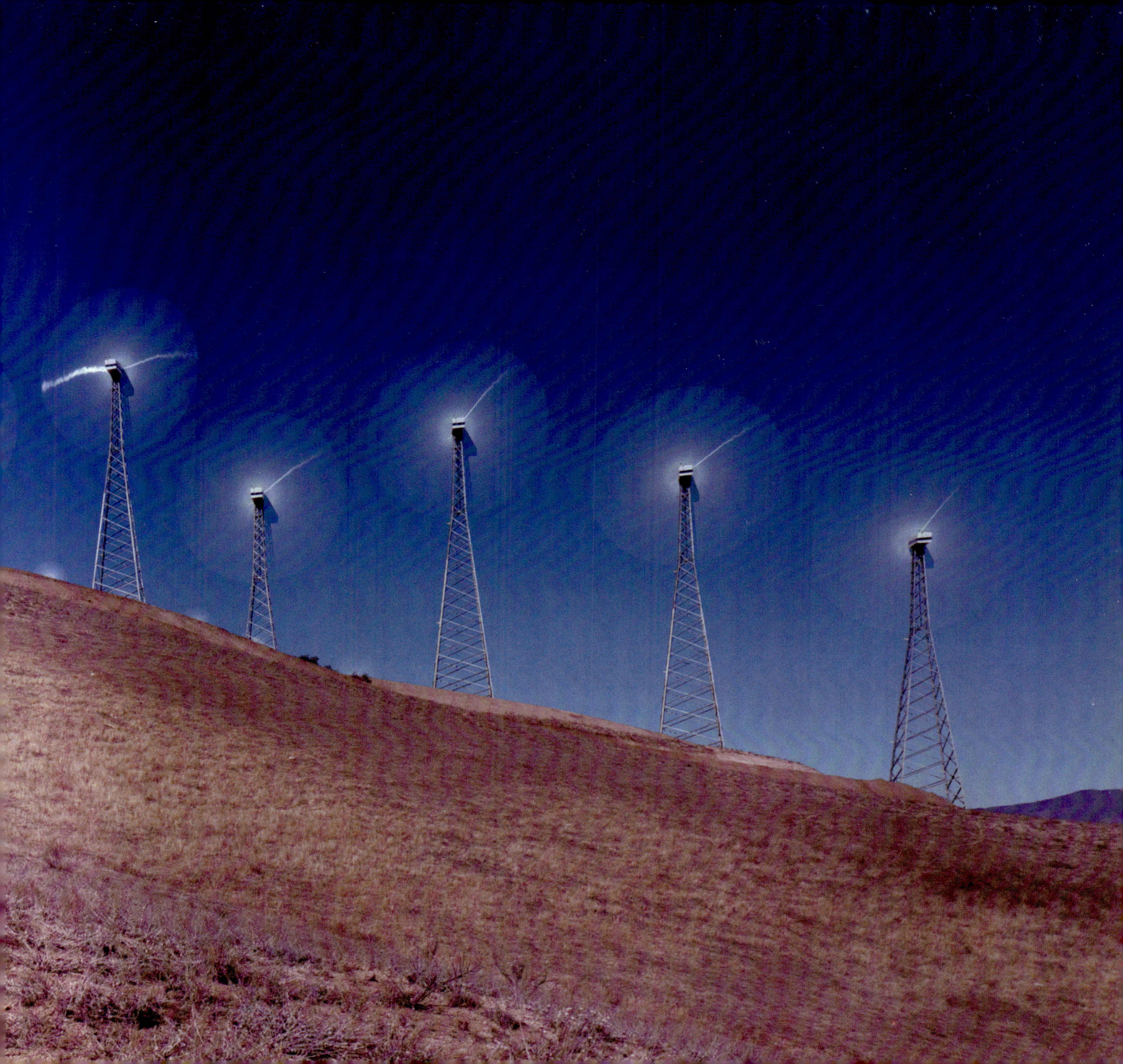

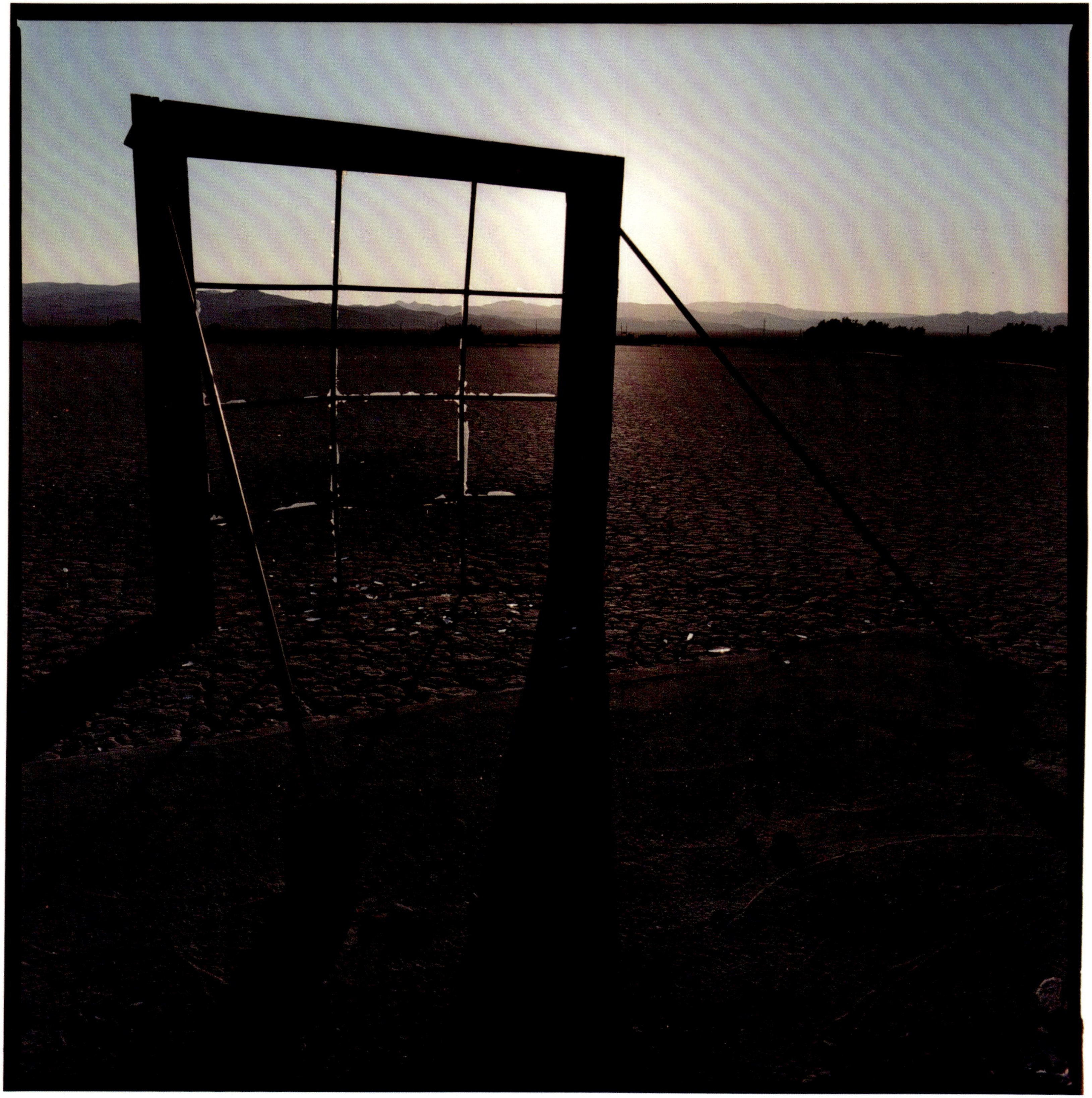

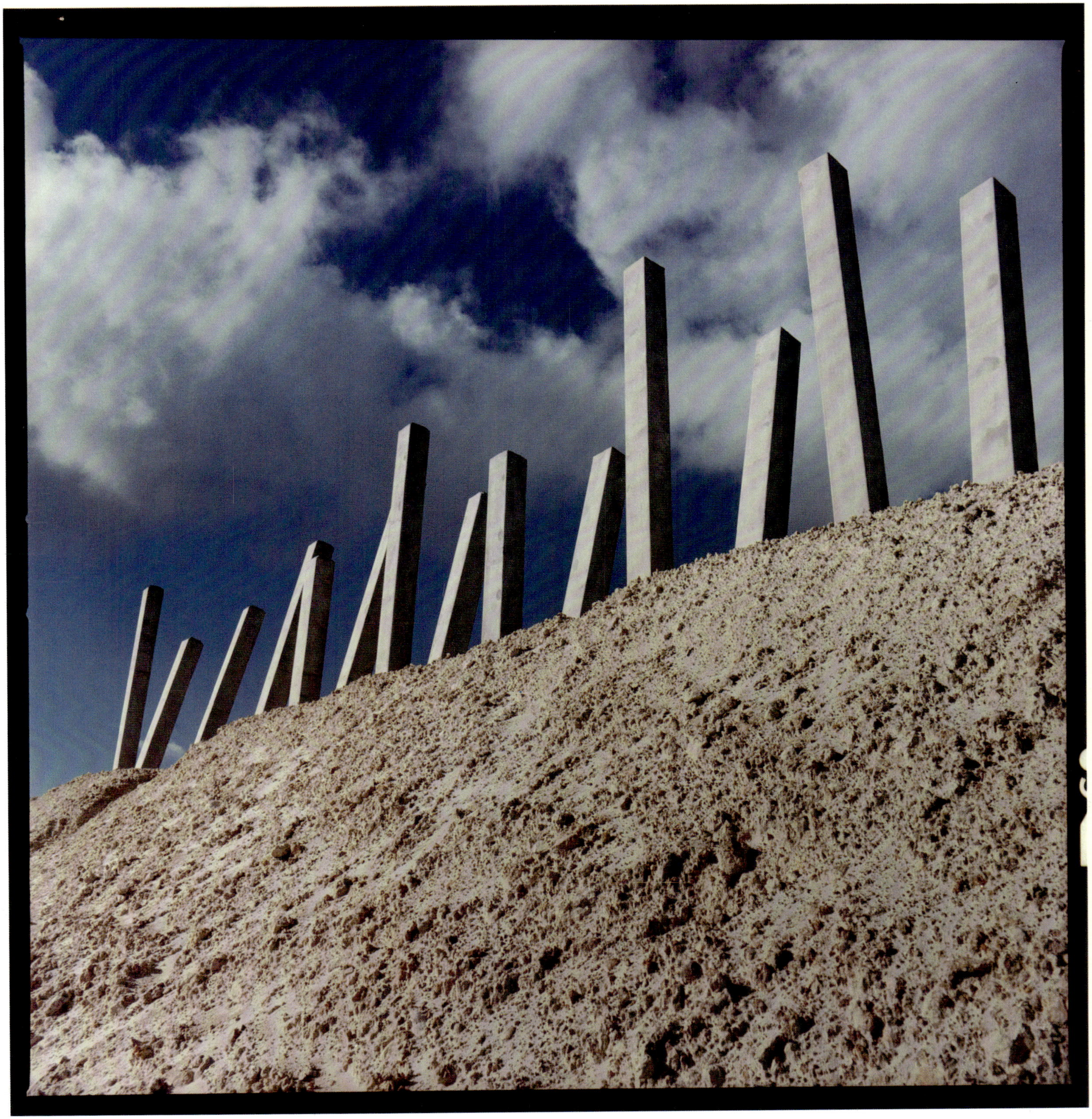

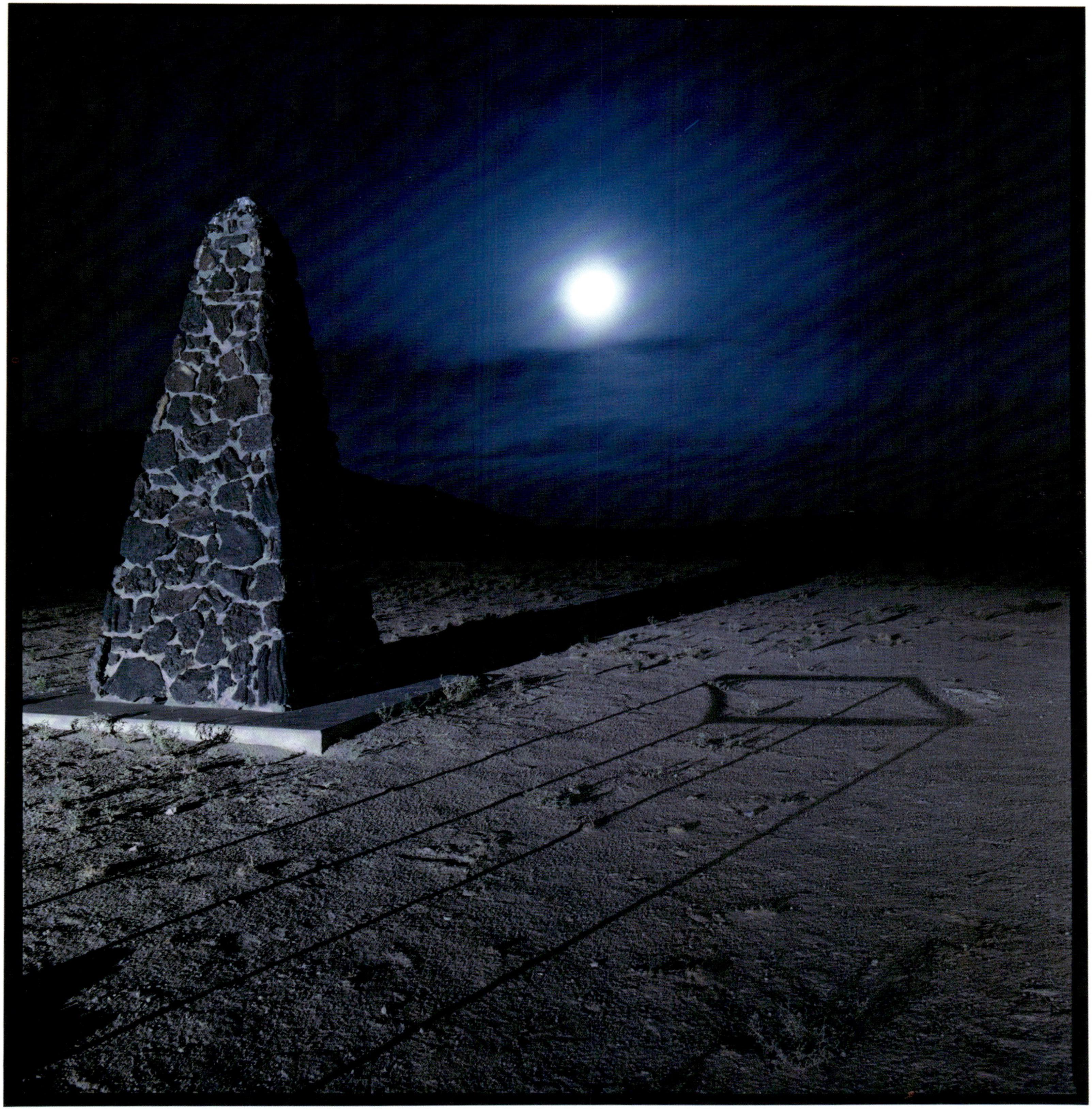

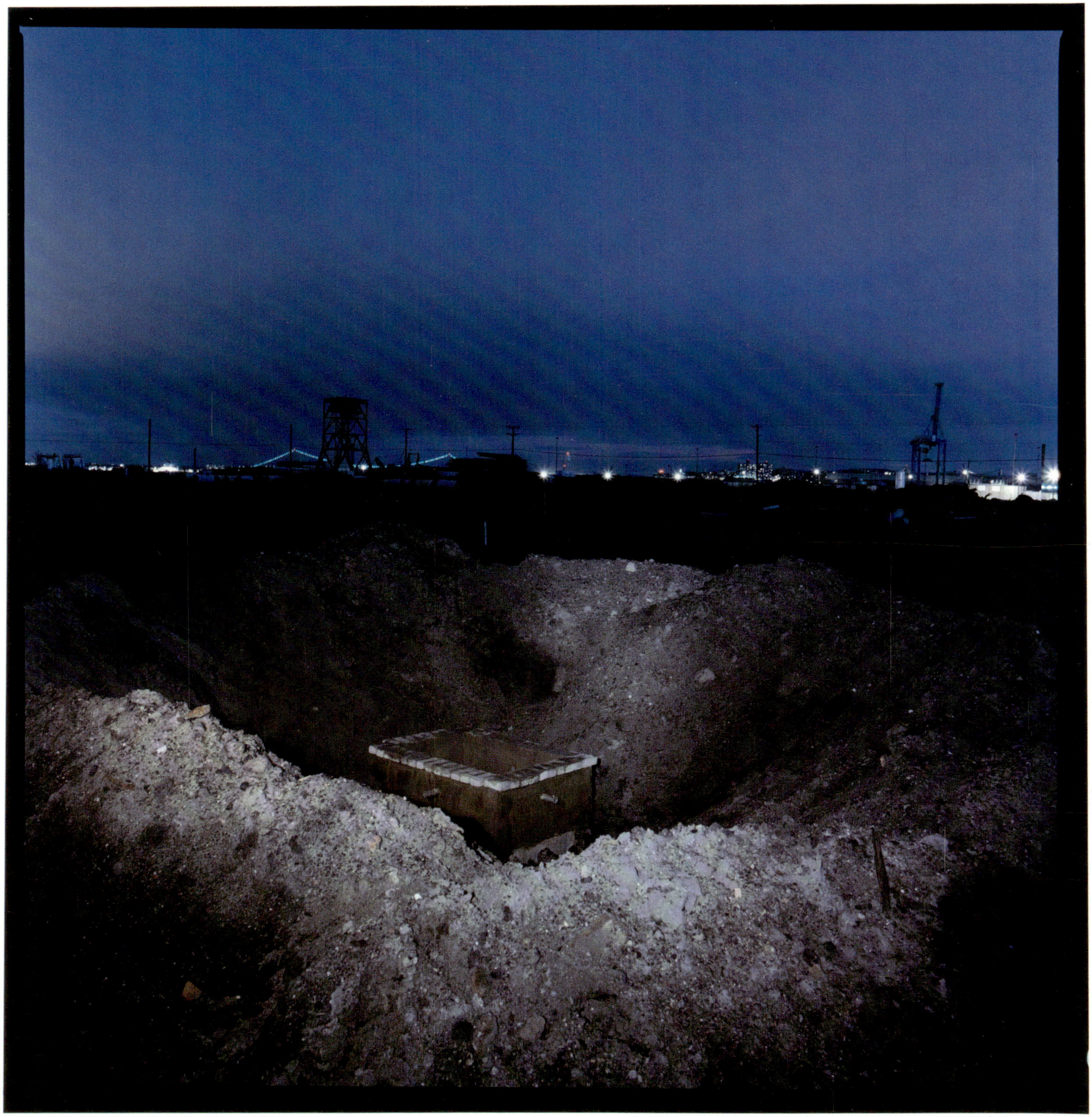

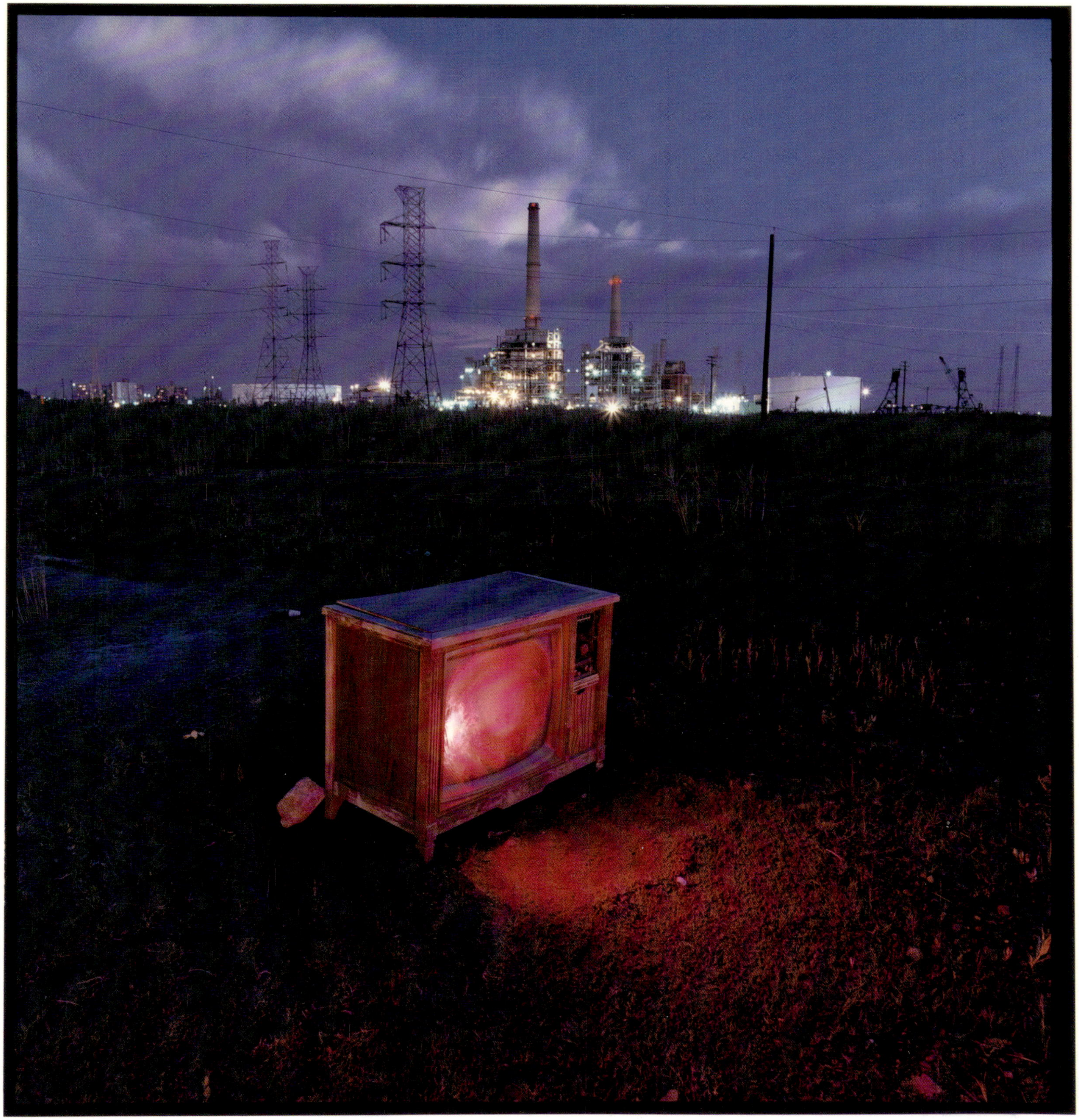

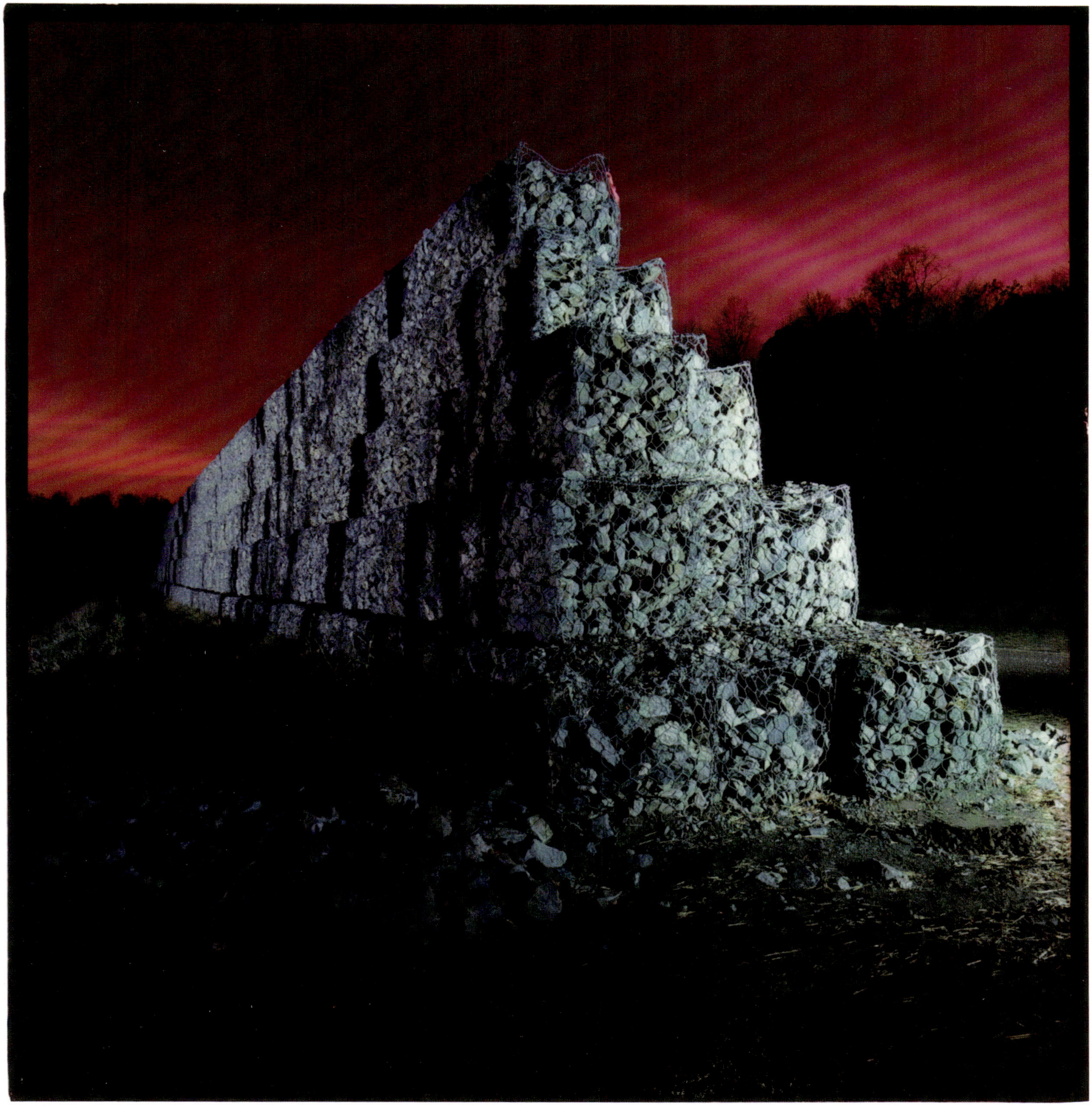

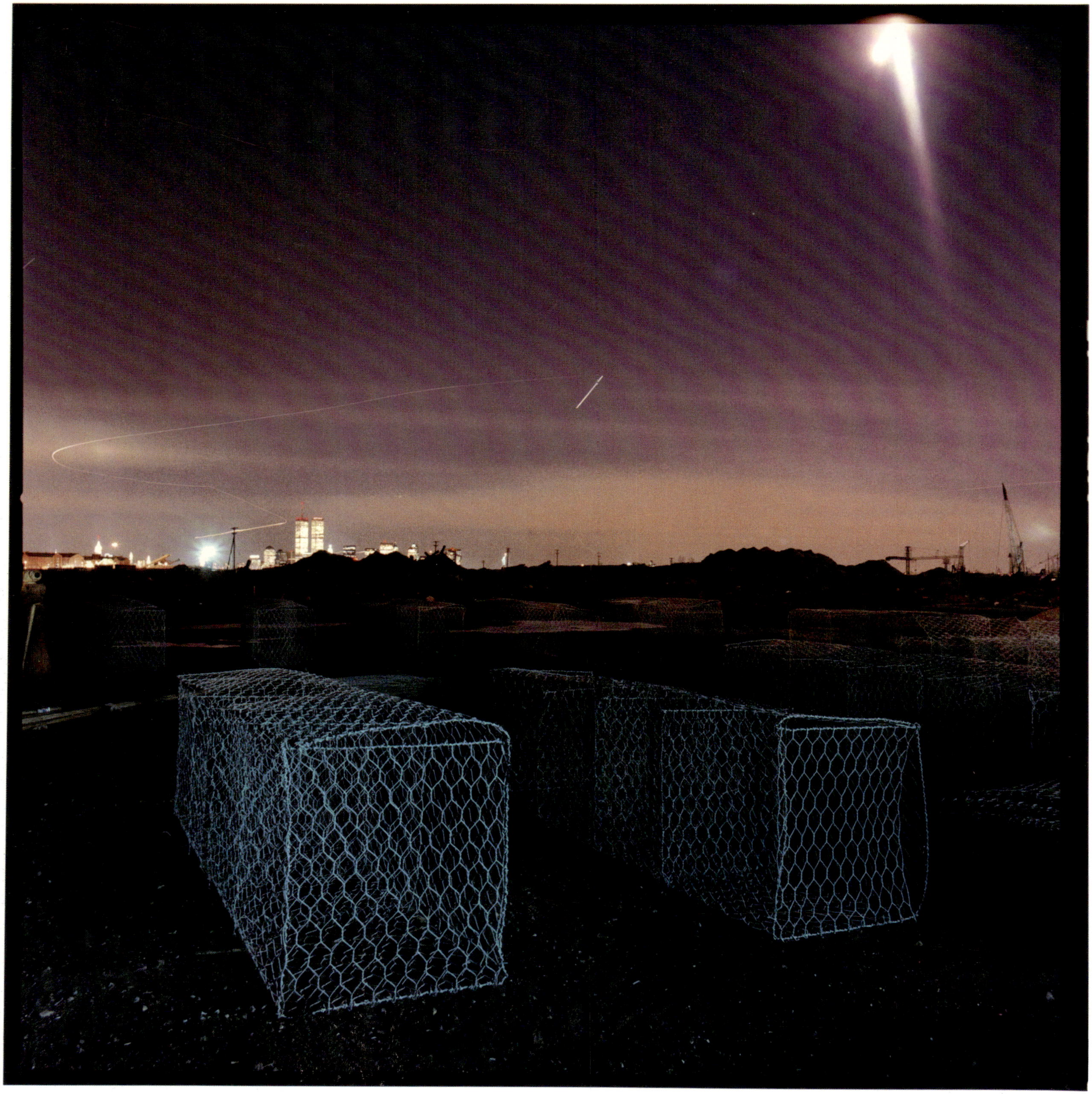

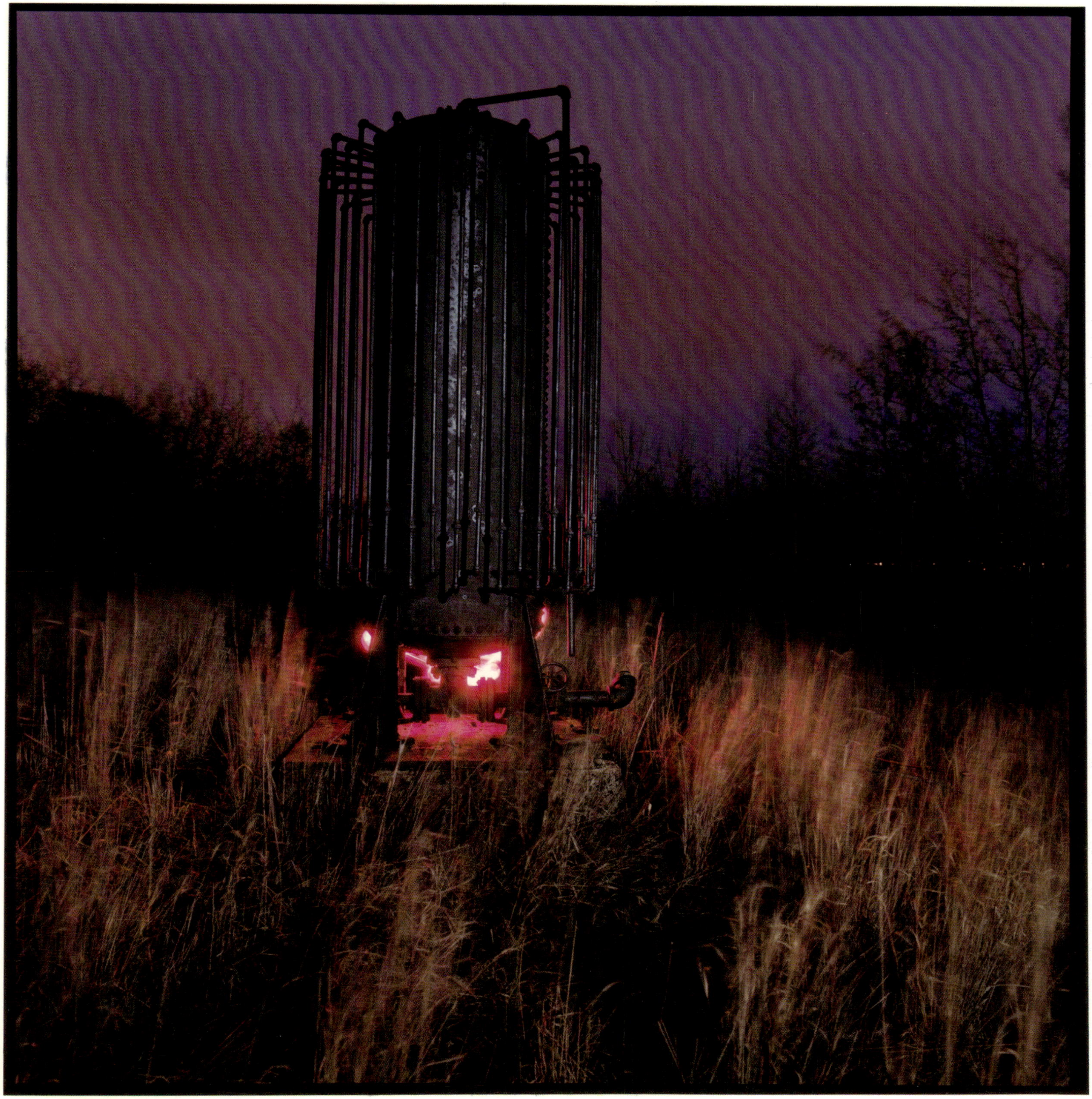

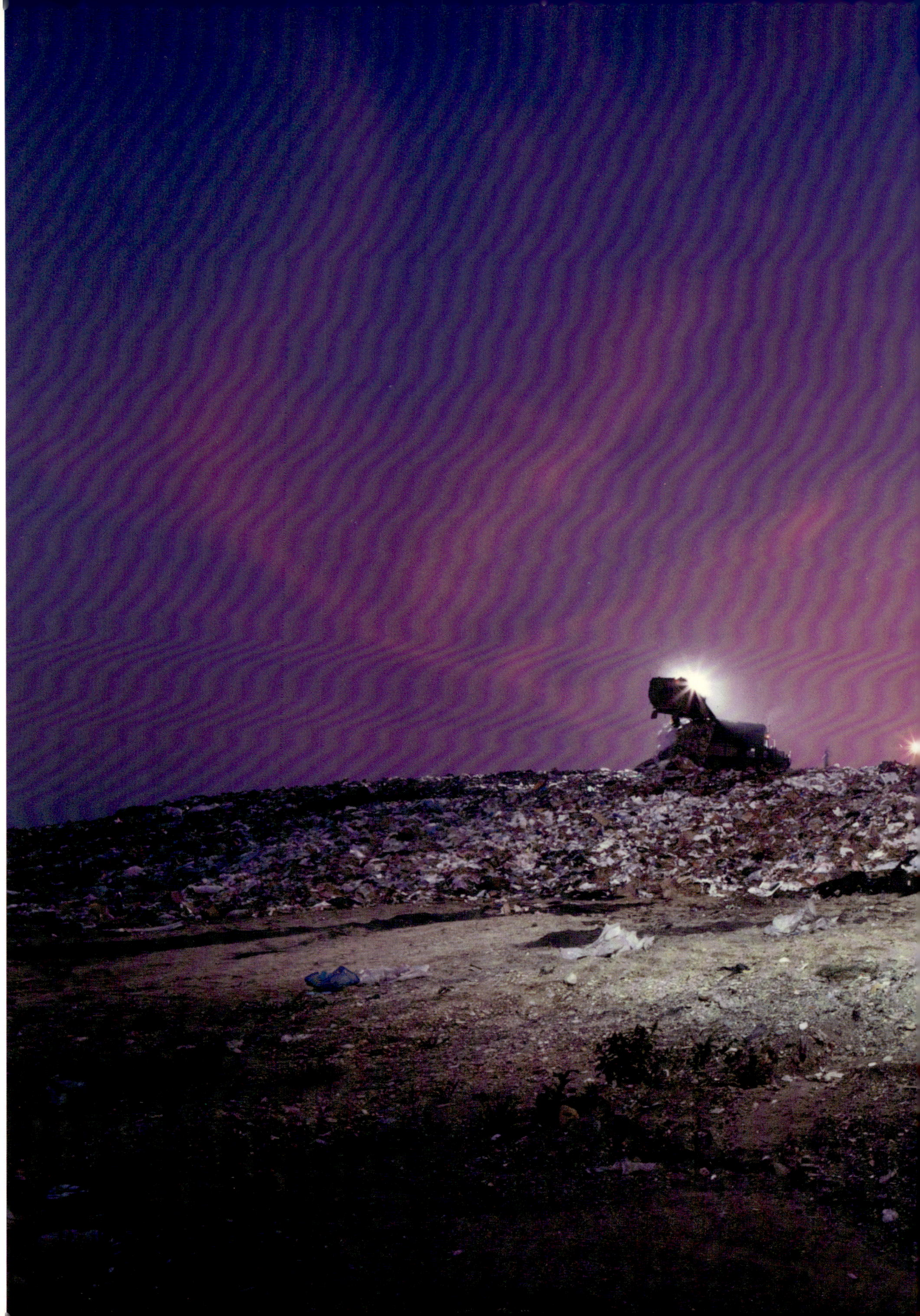

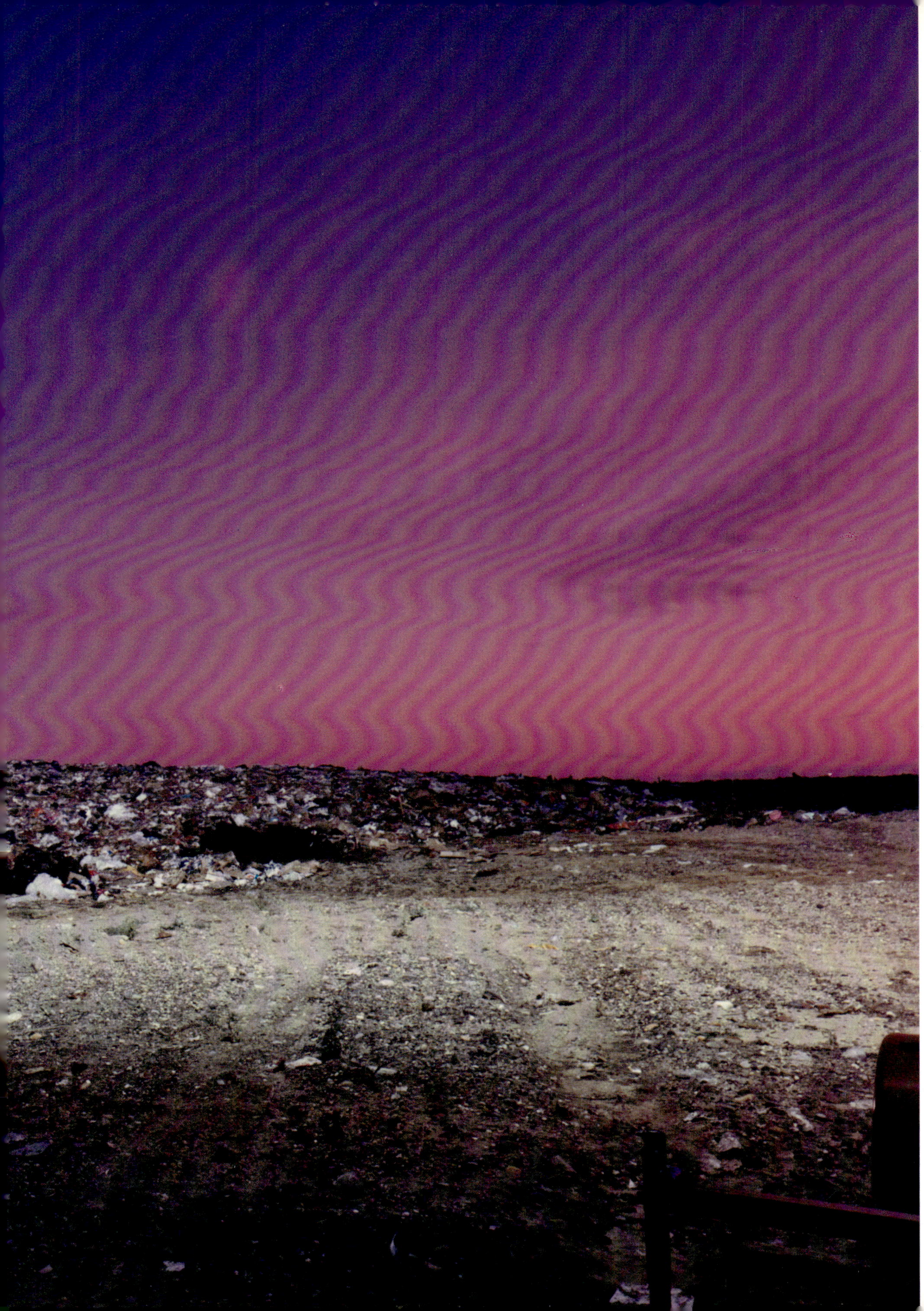

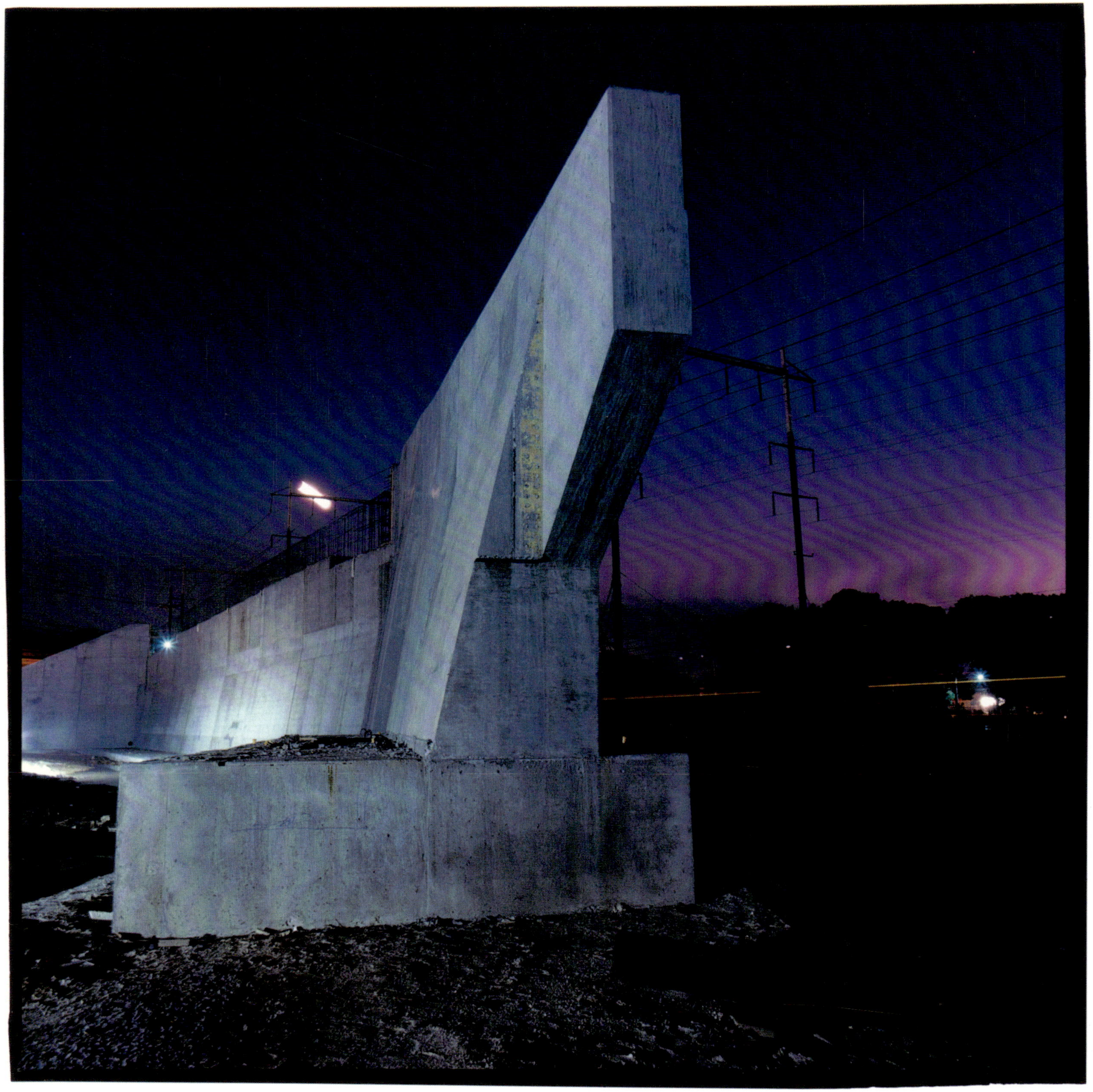

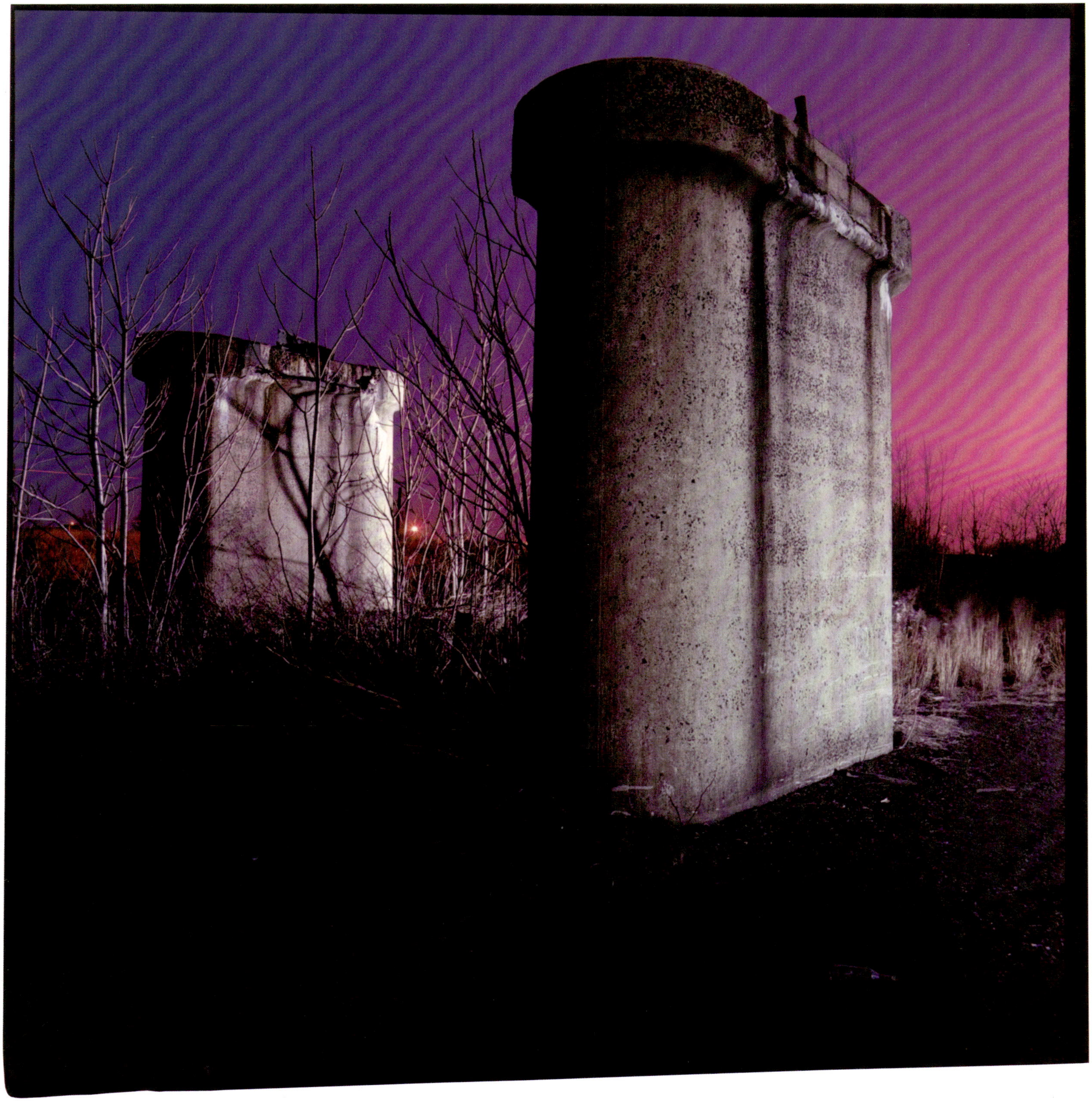

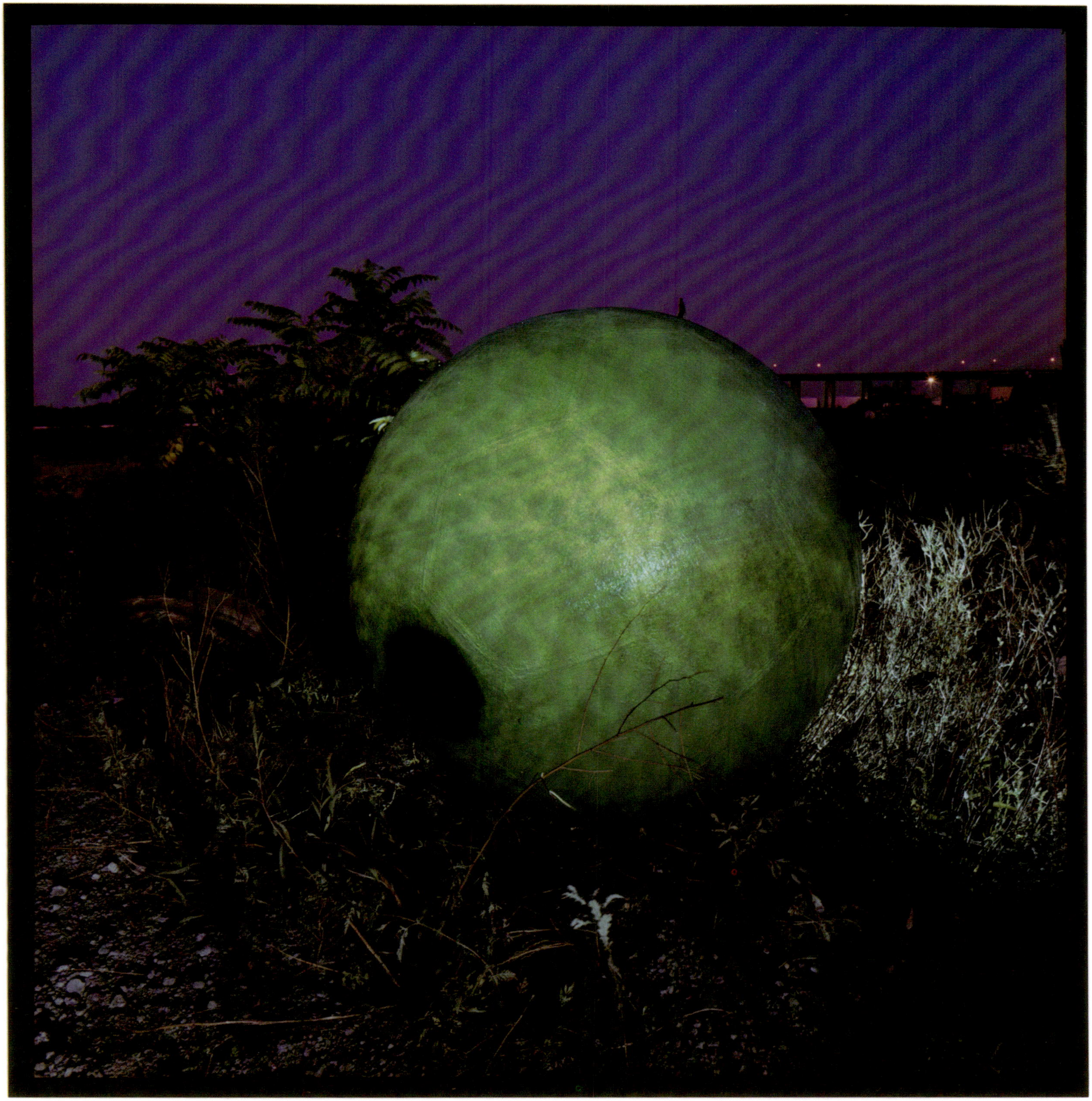

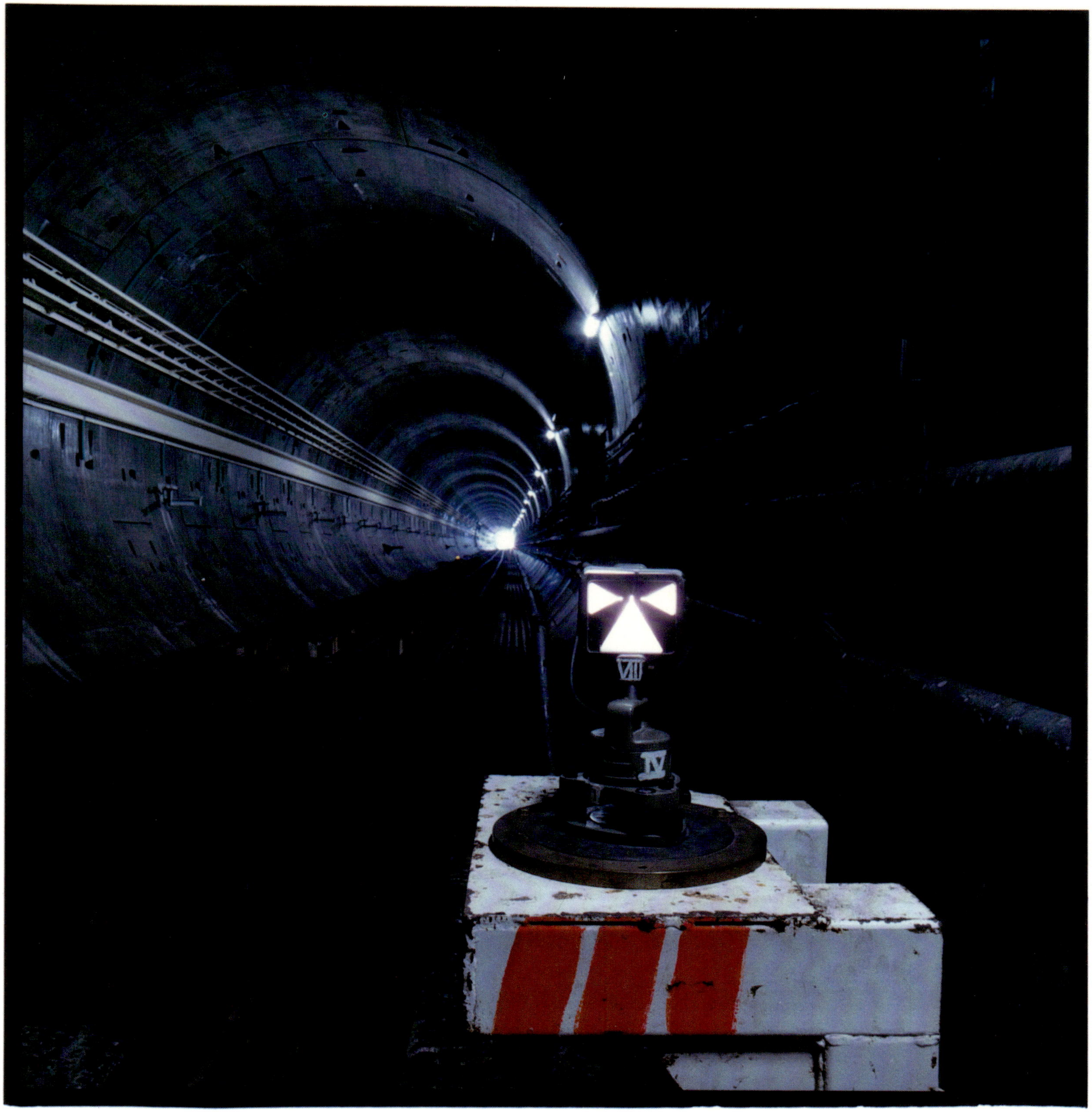
IV

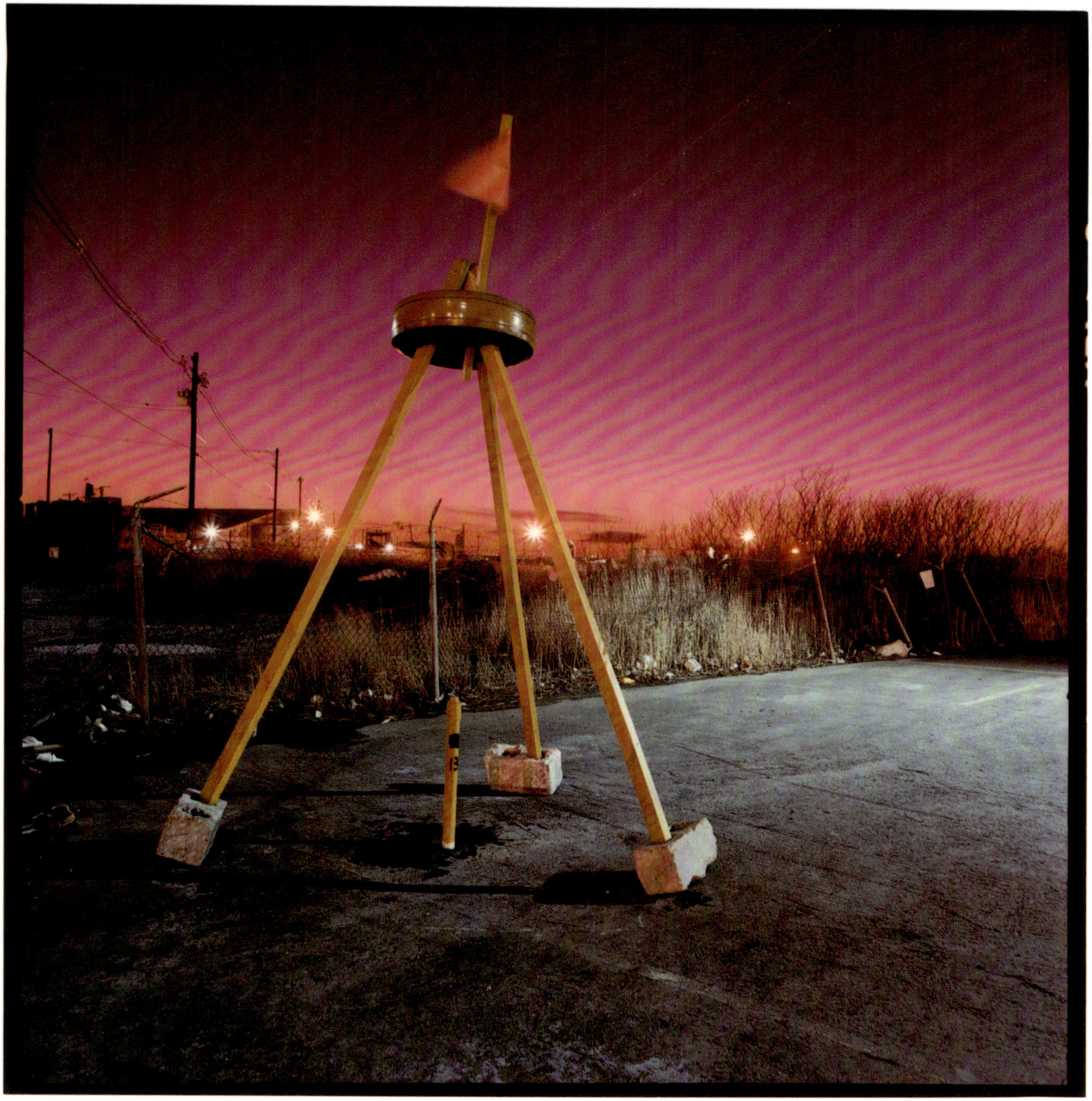

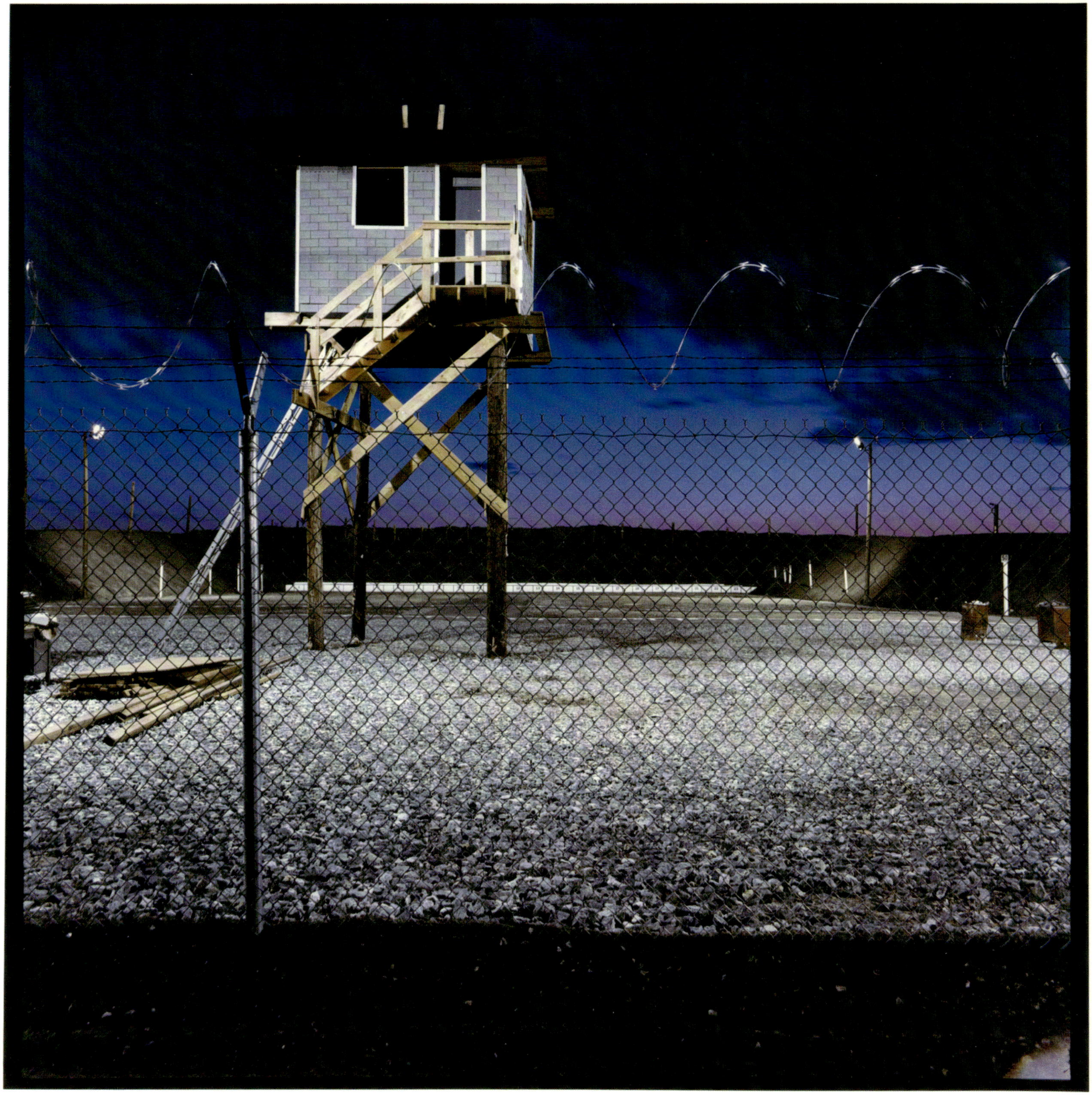

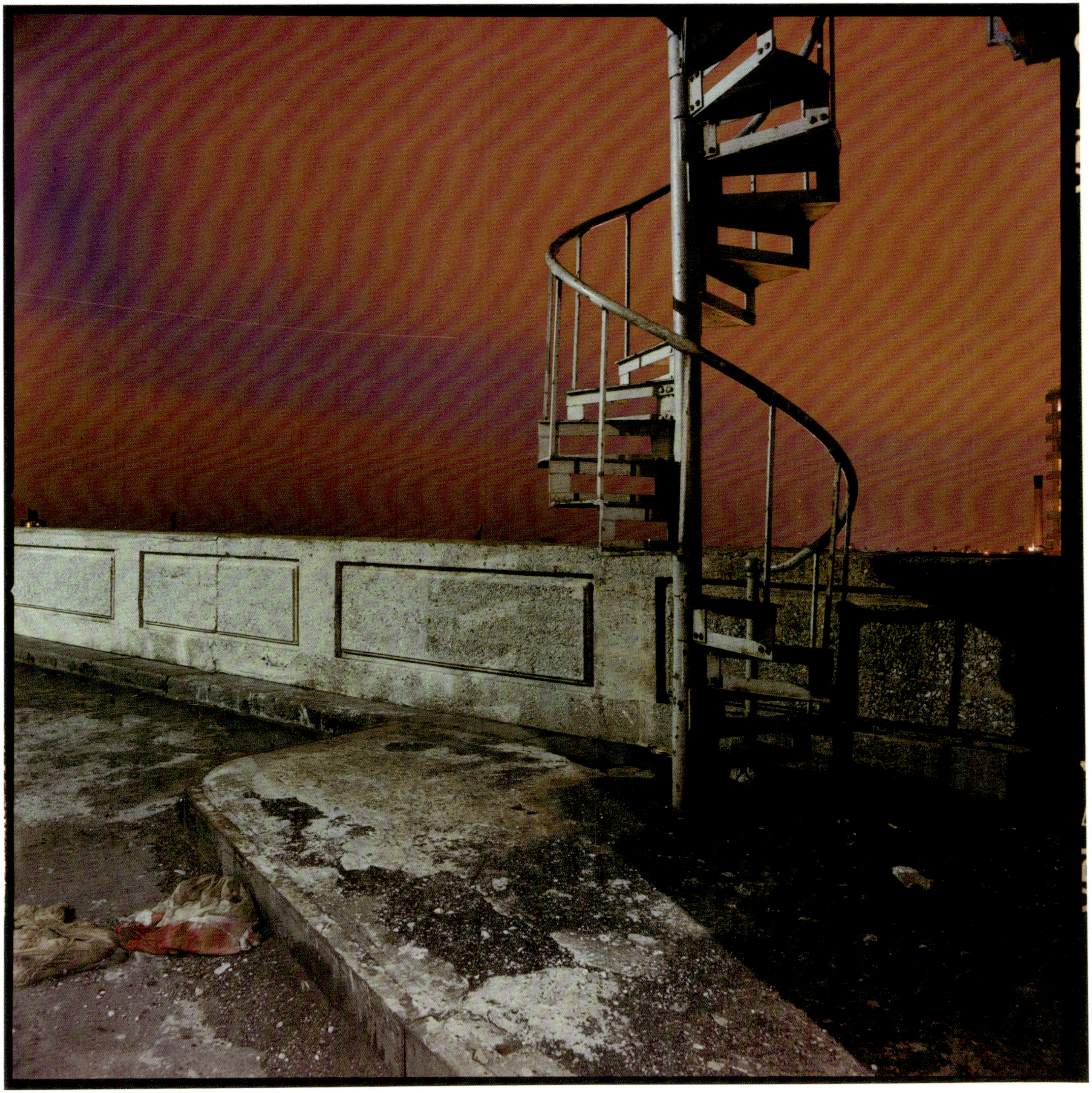

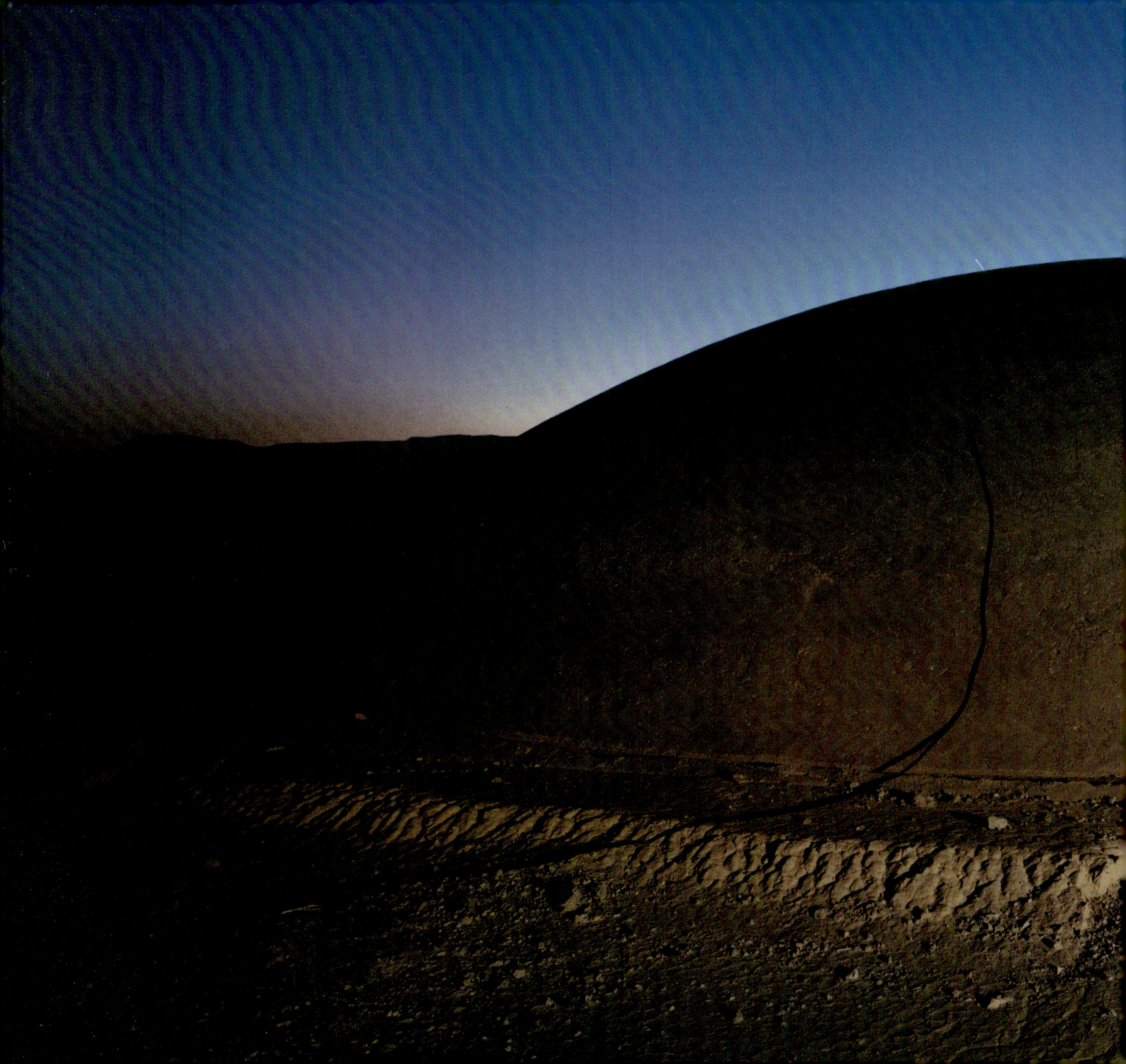

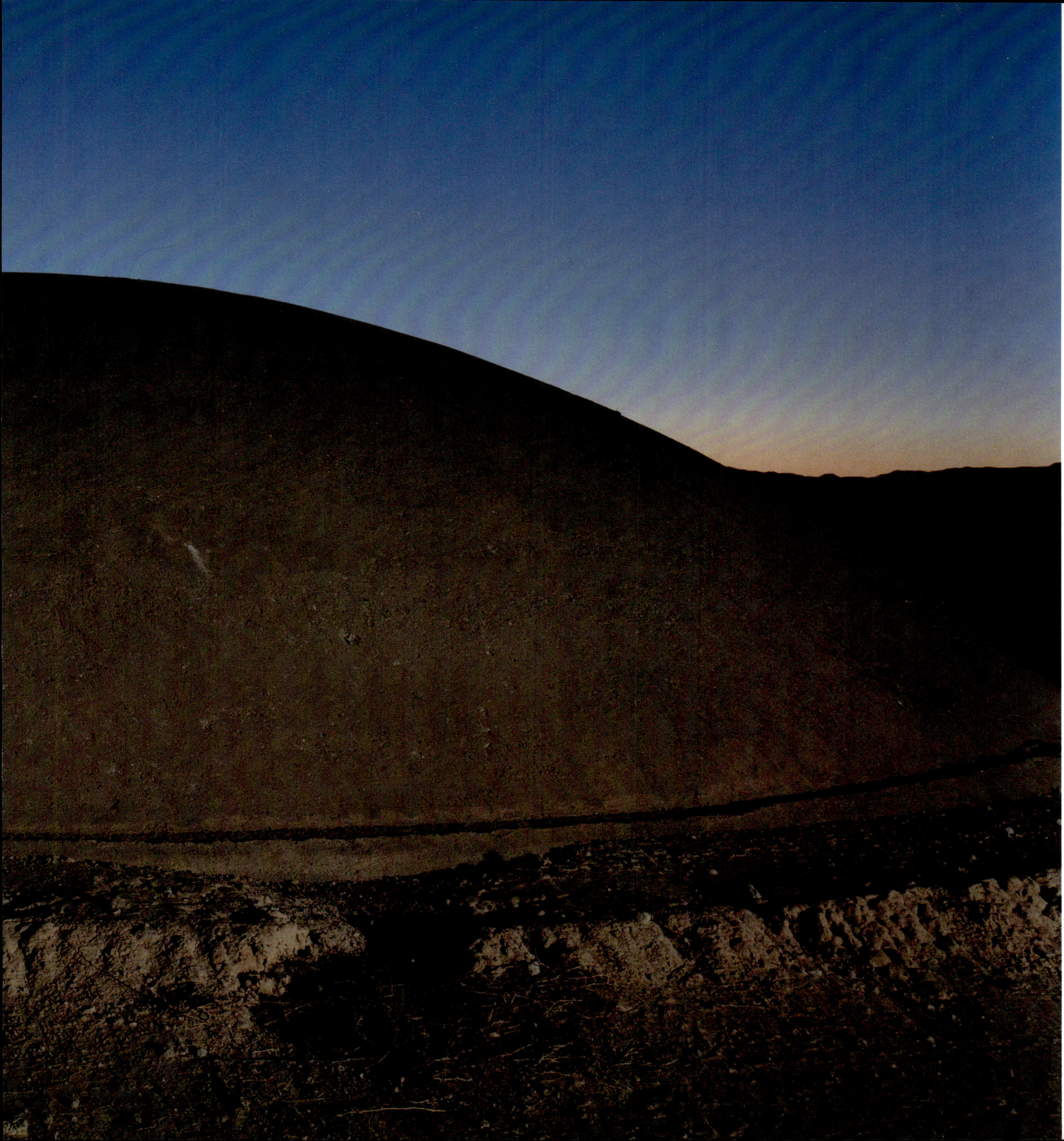

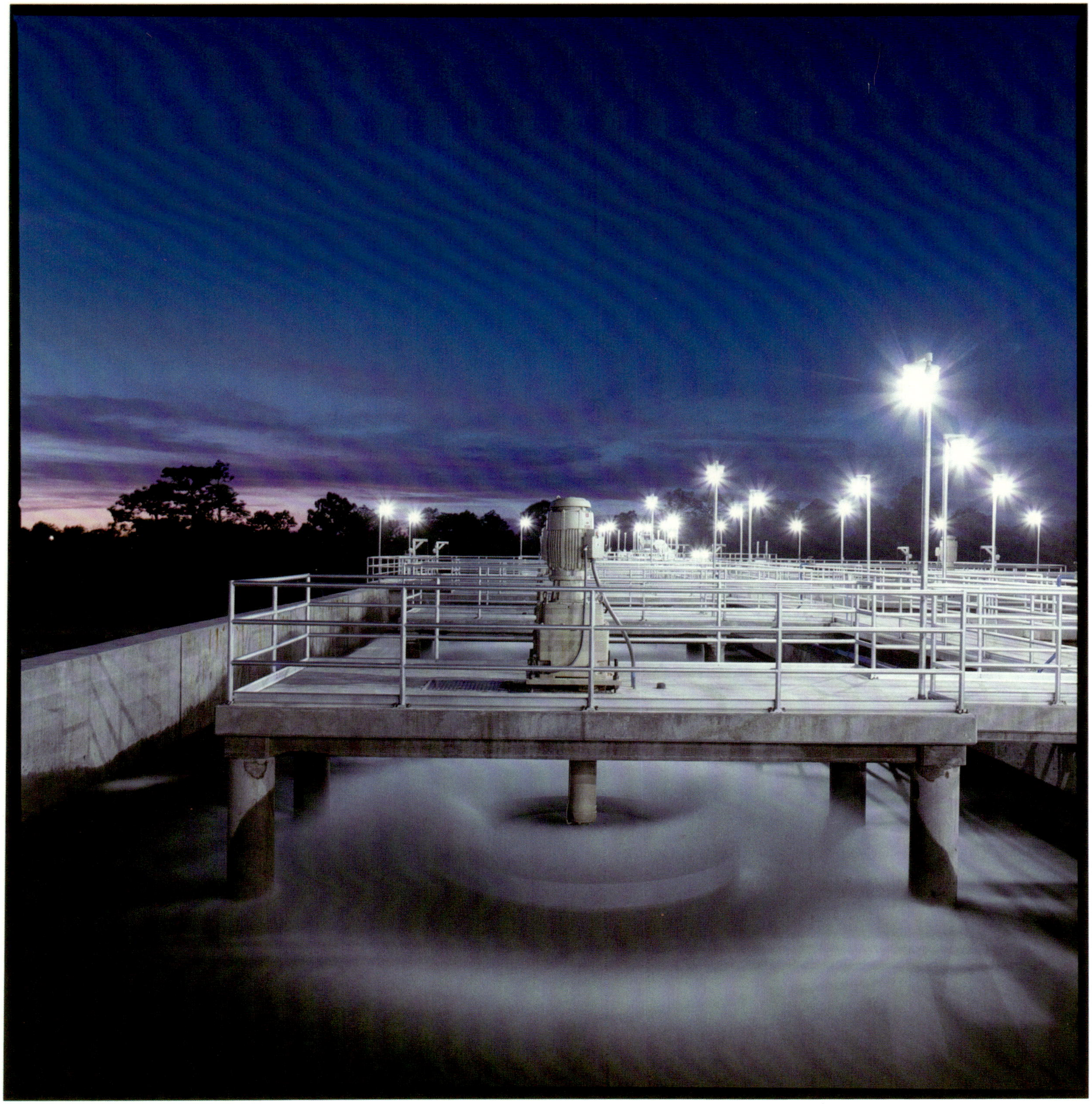

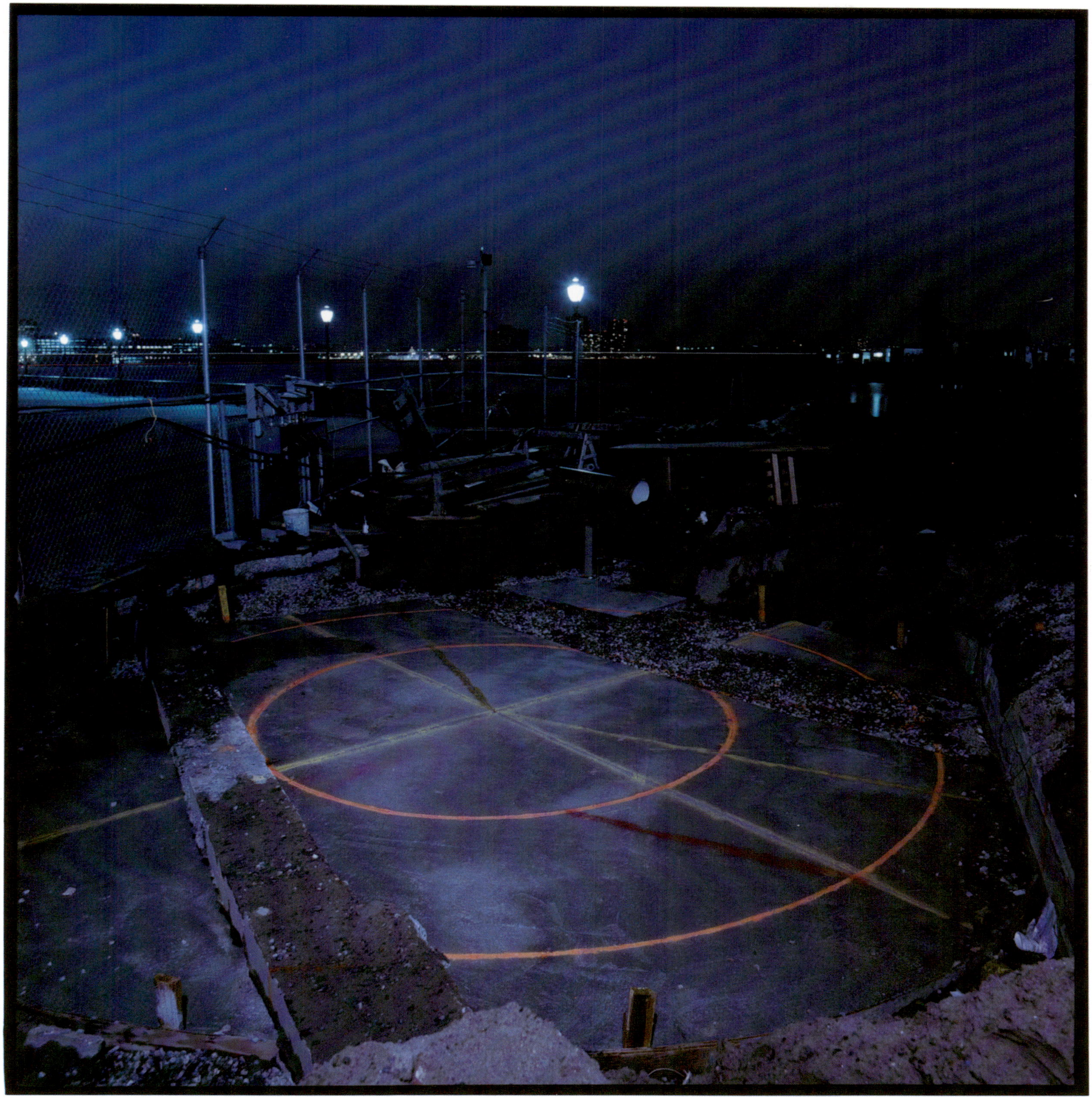

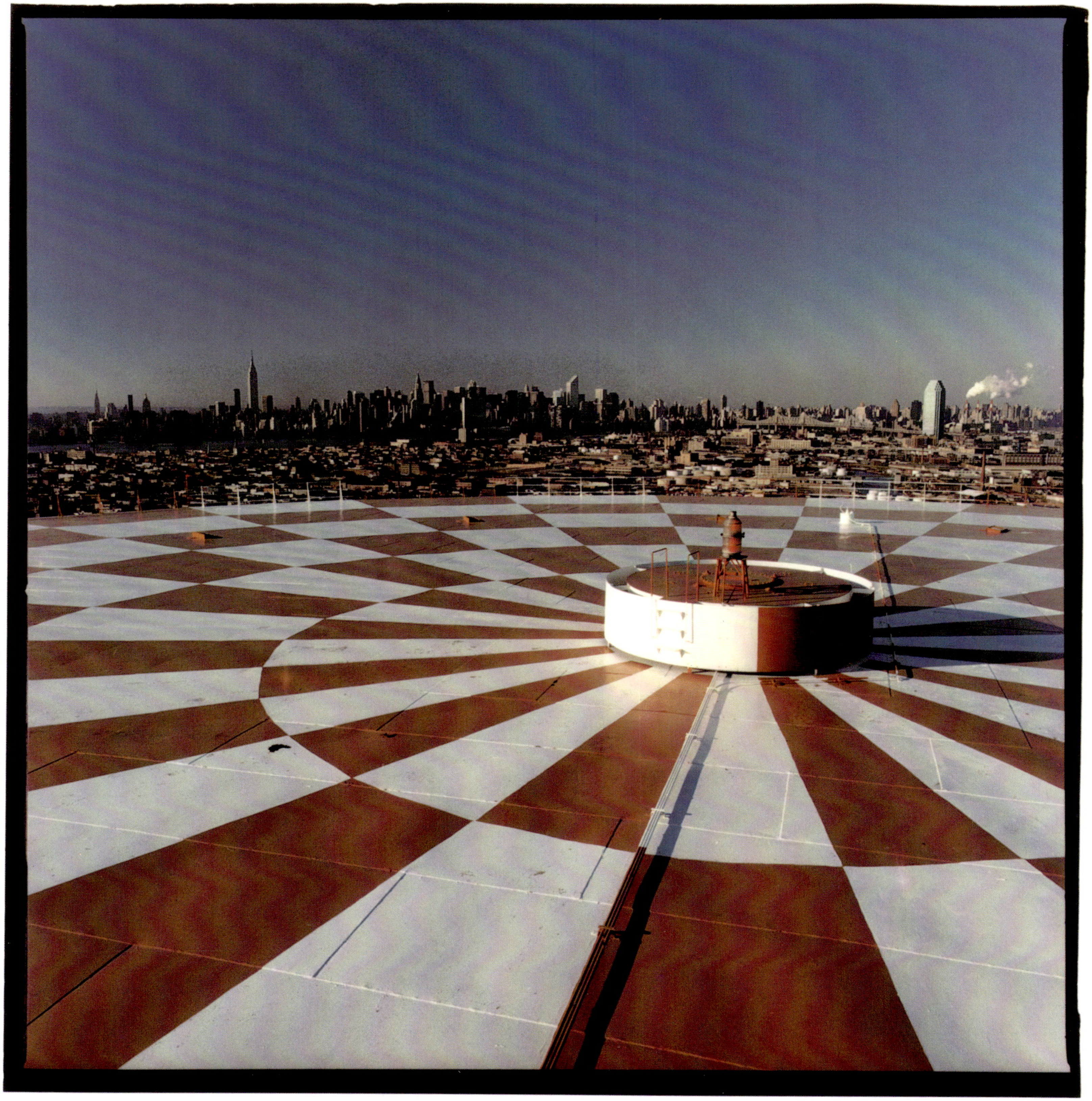

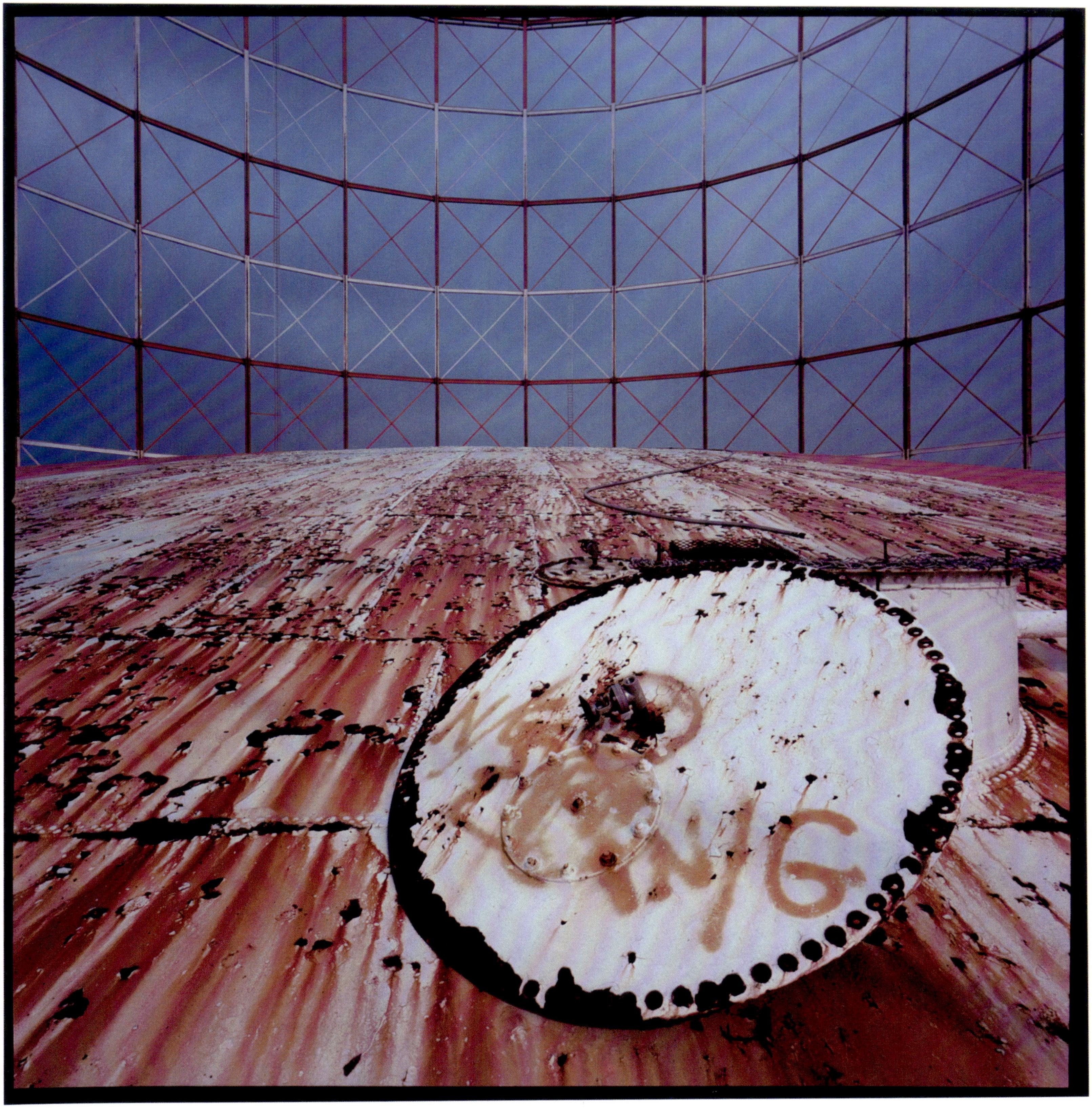

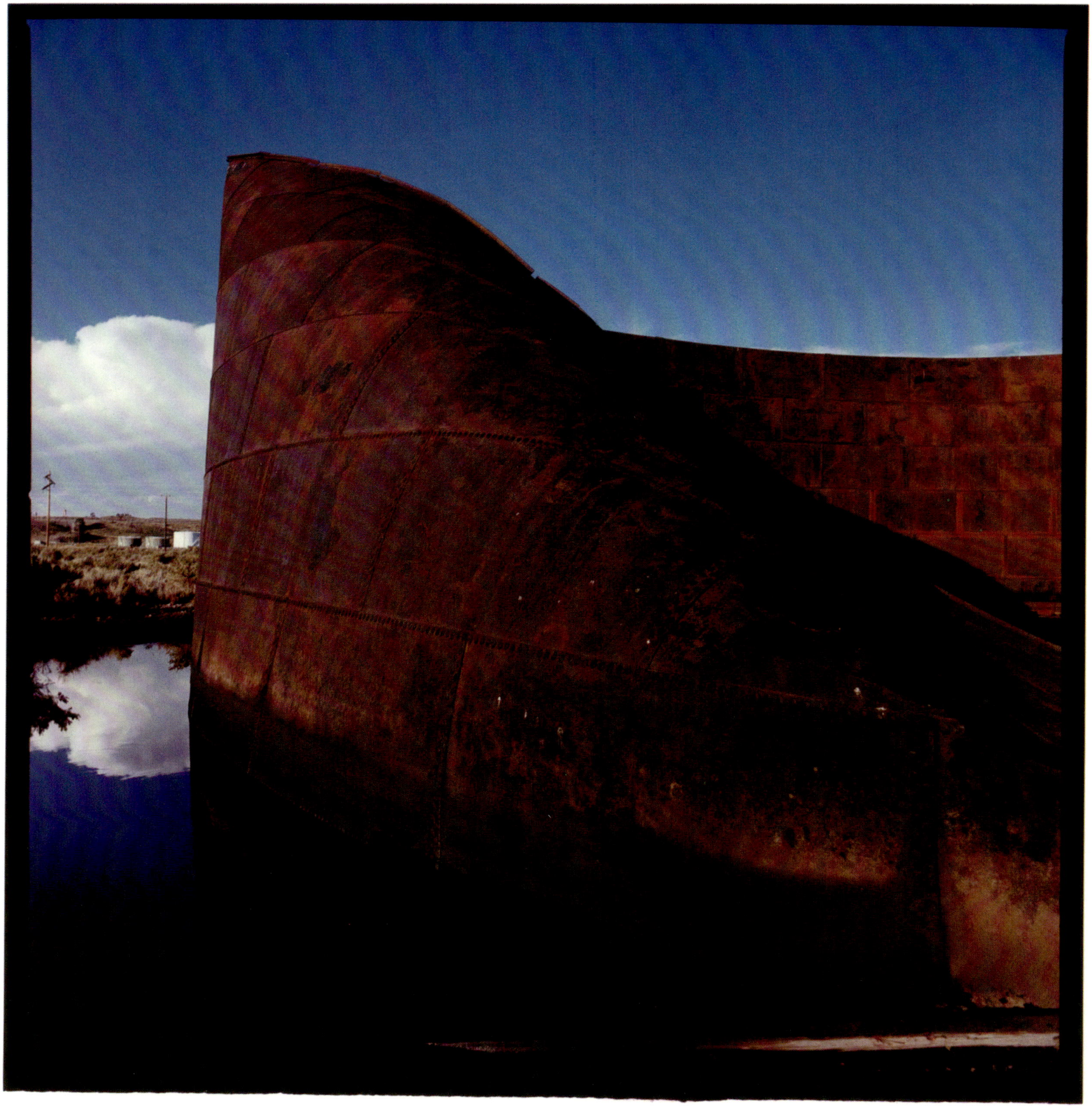

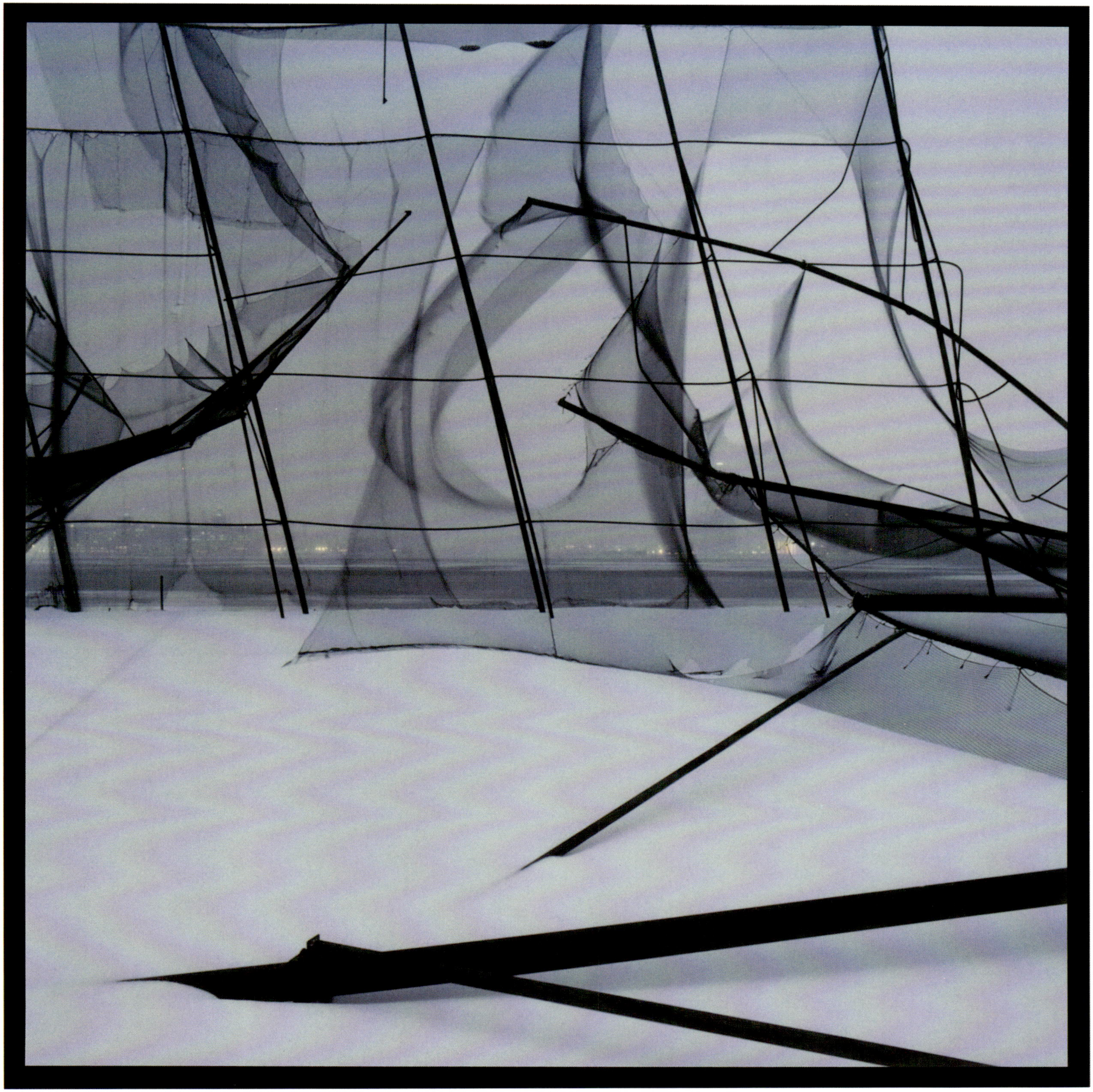

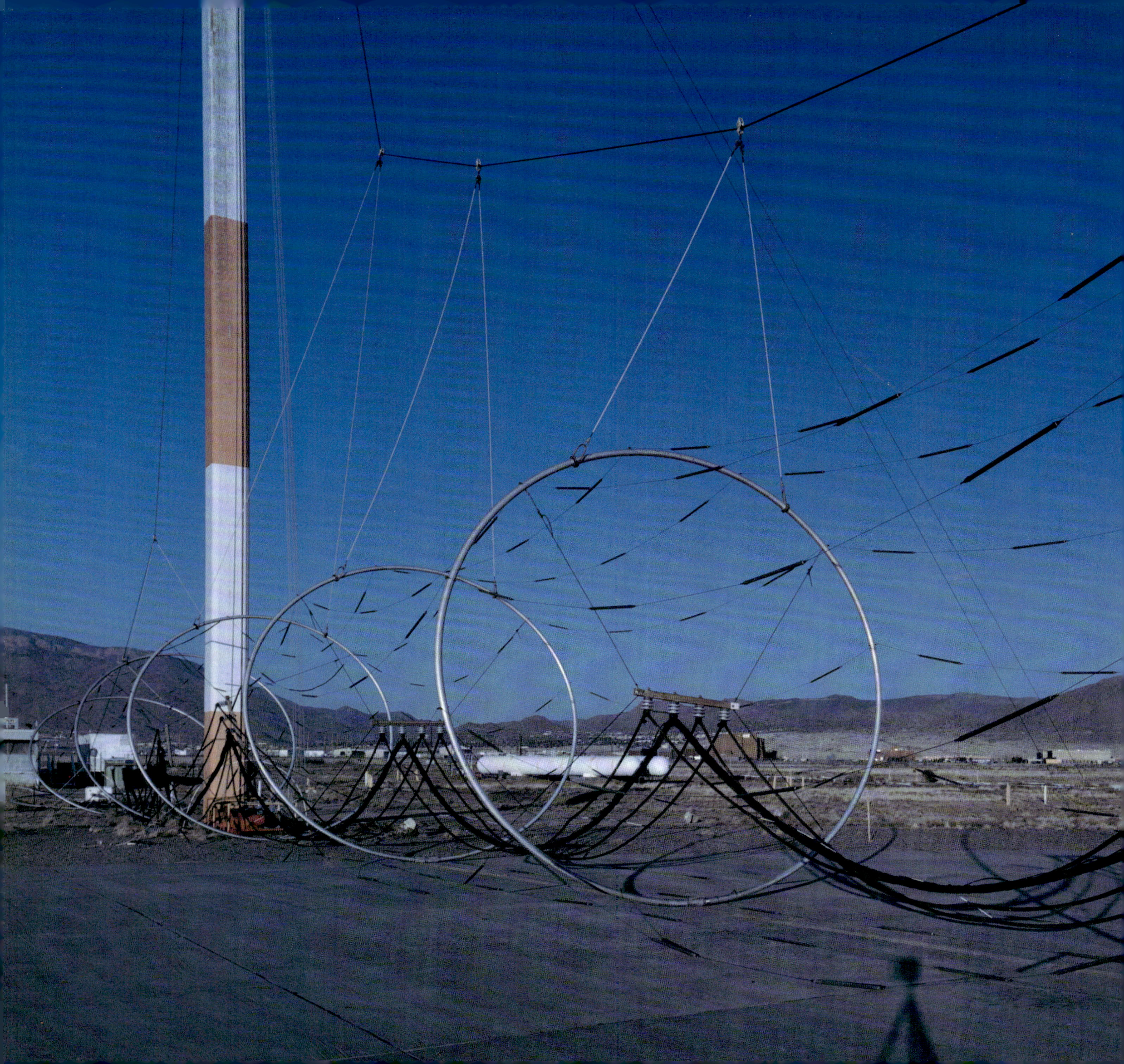

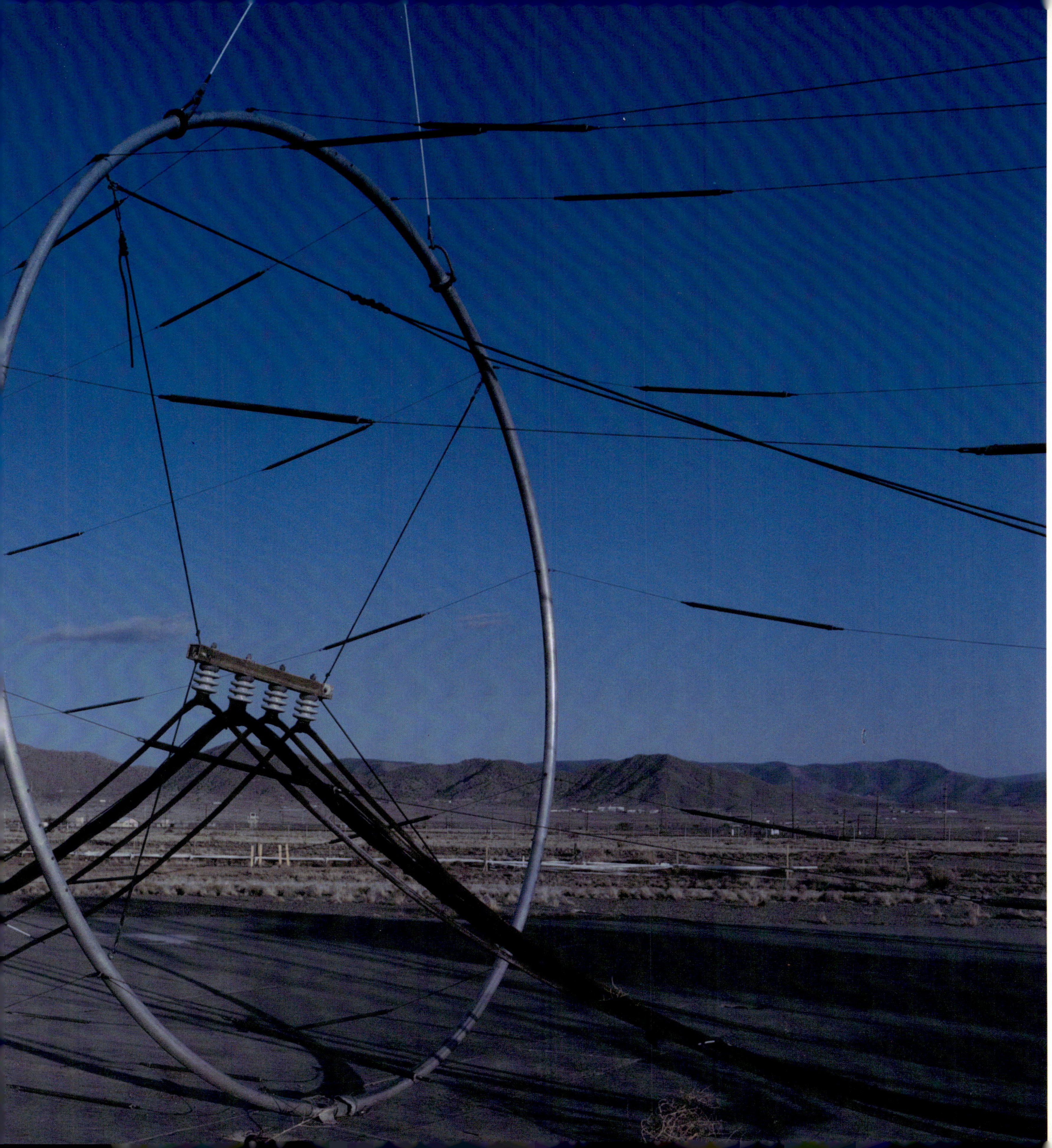

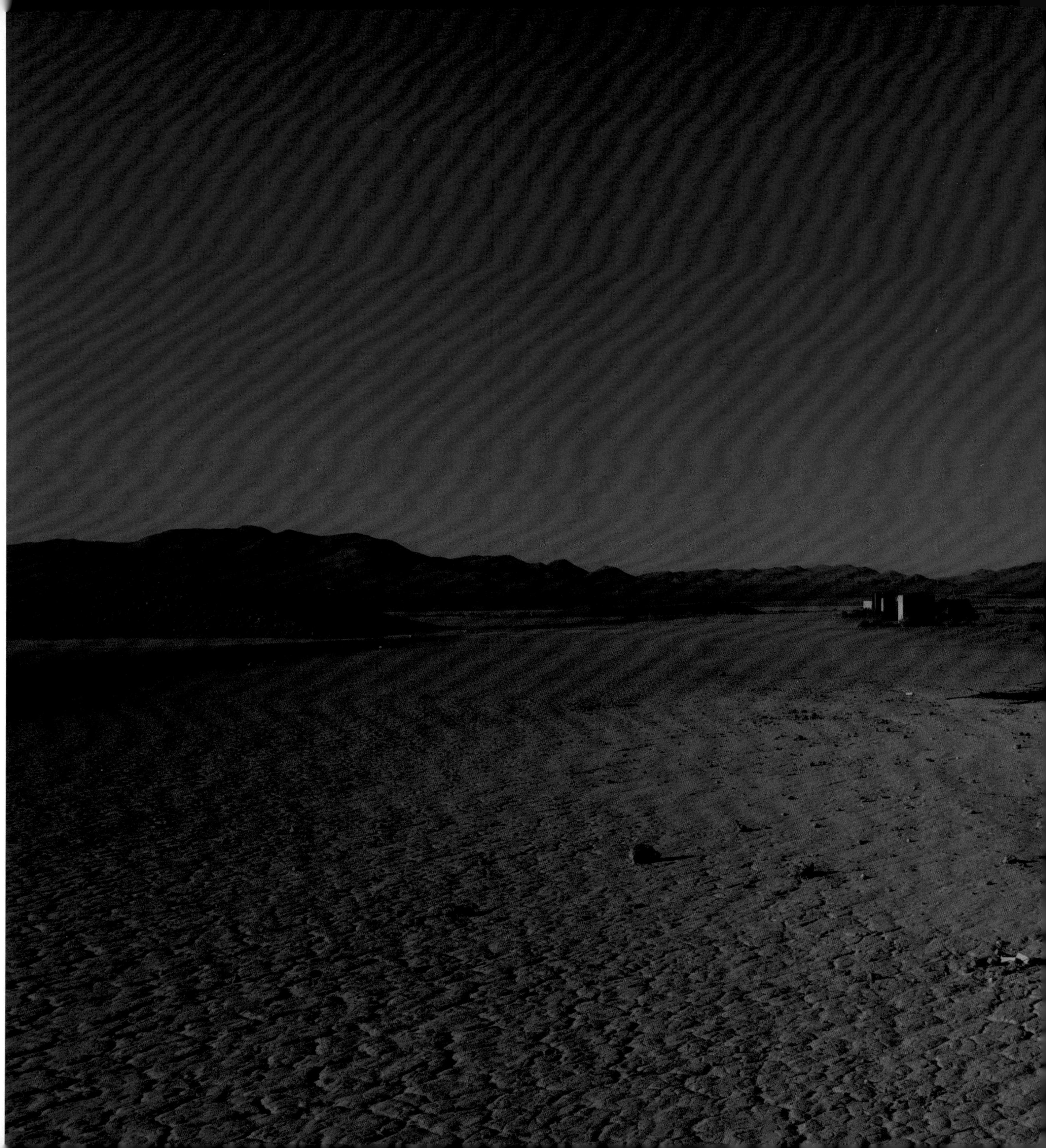

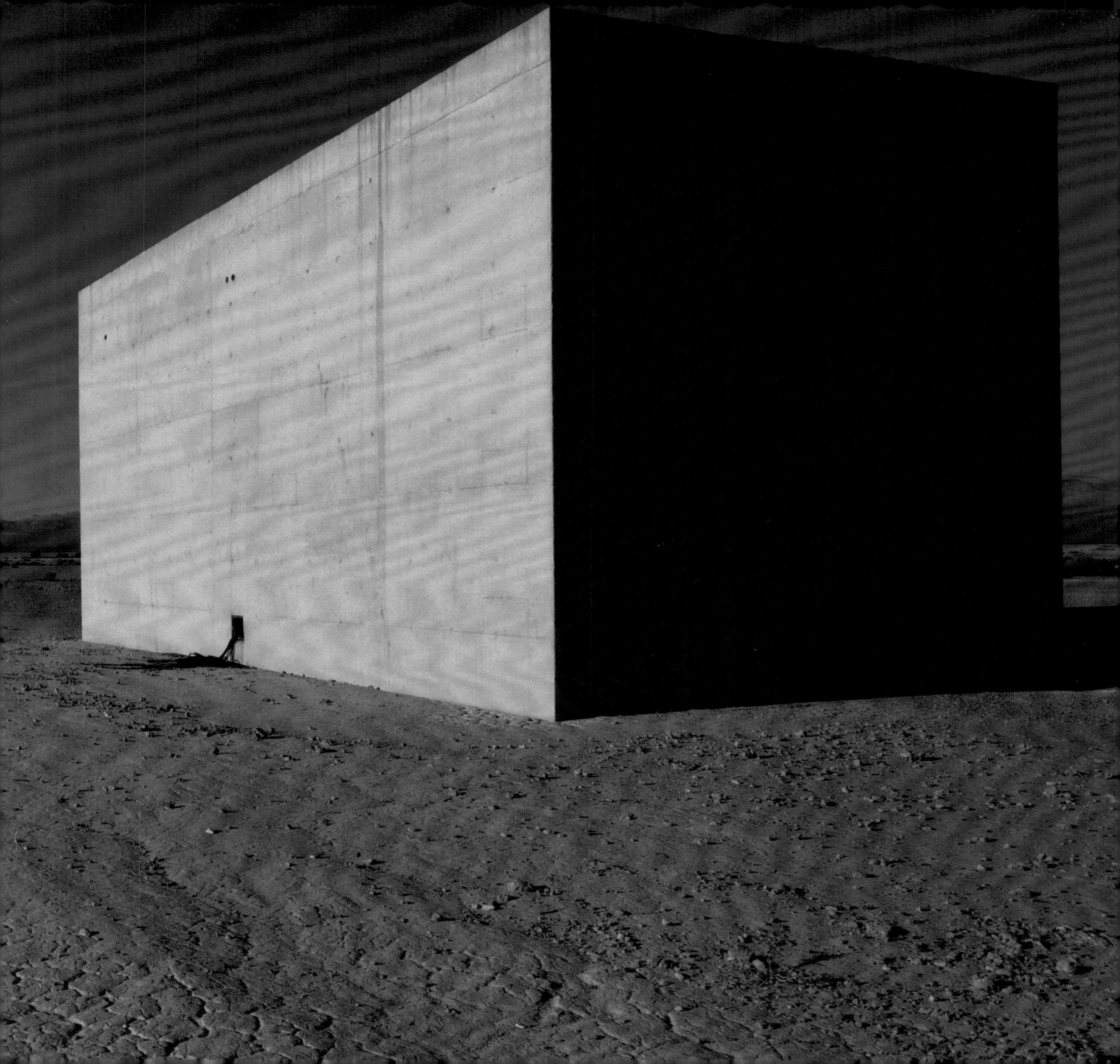

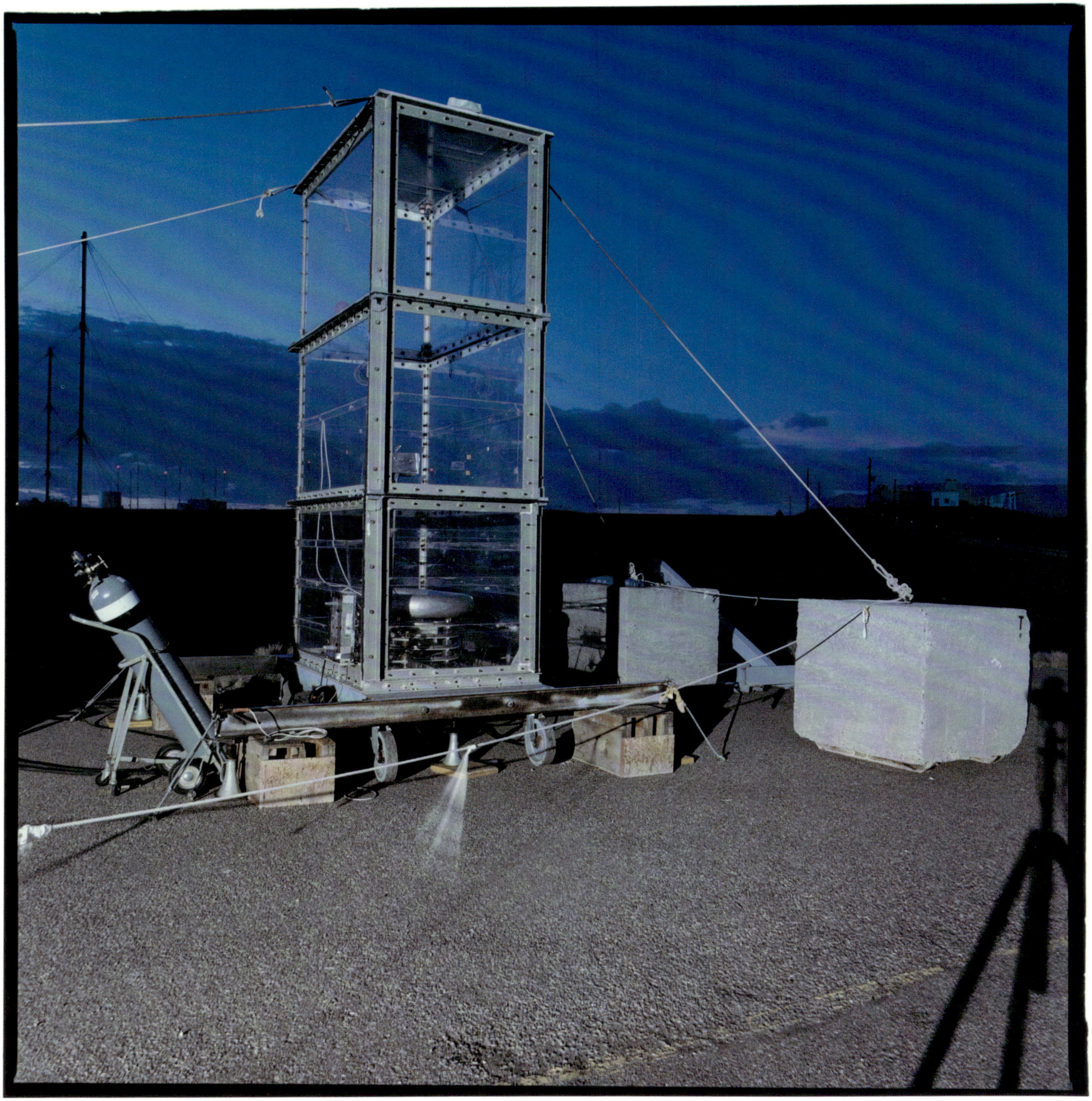

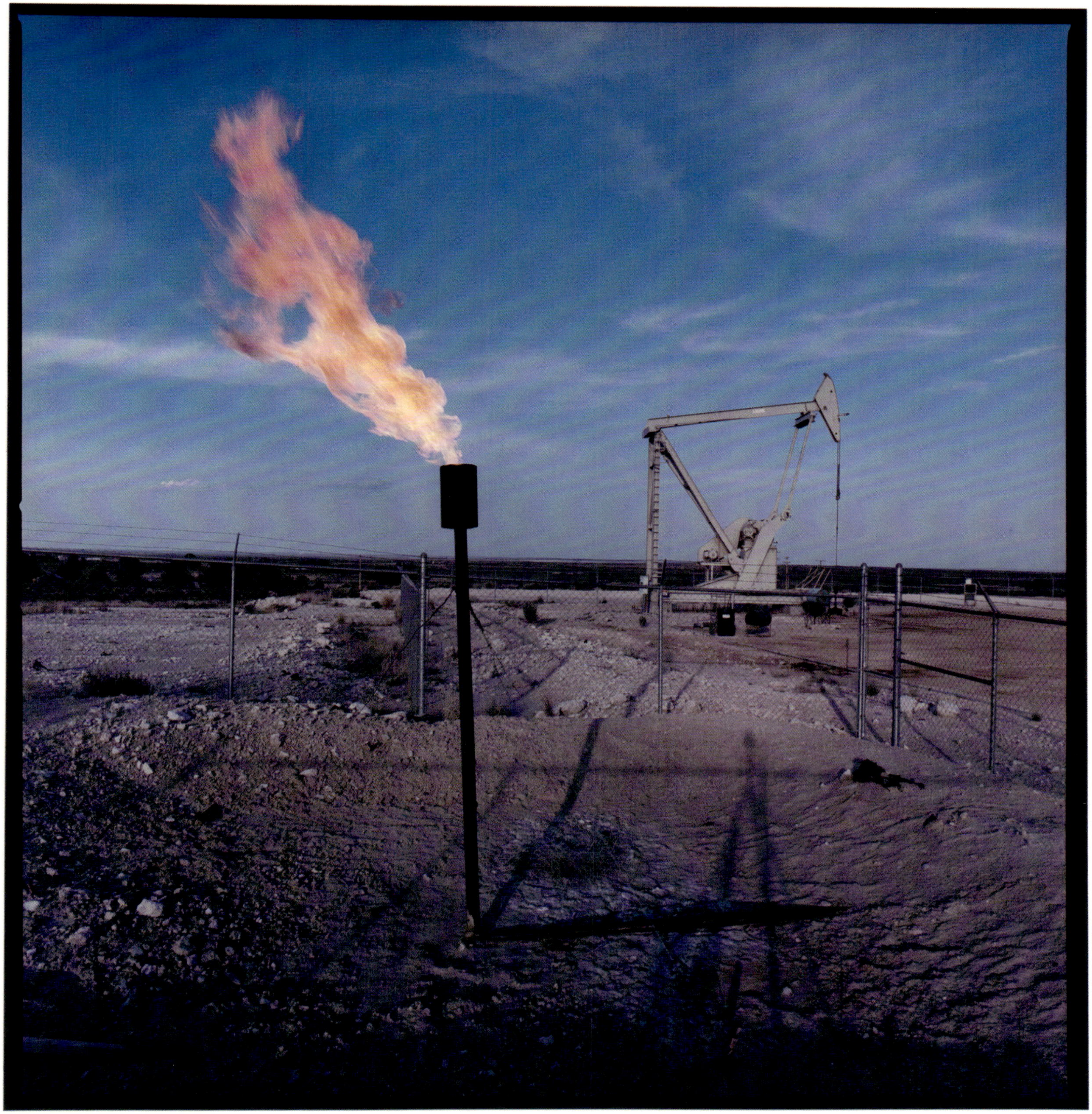

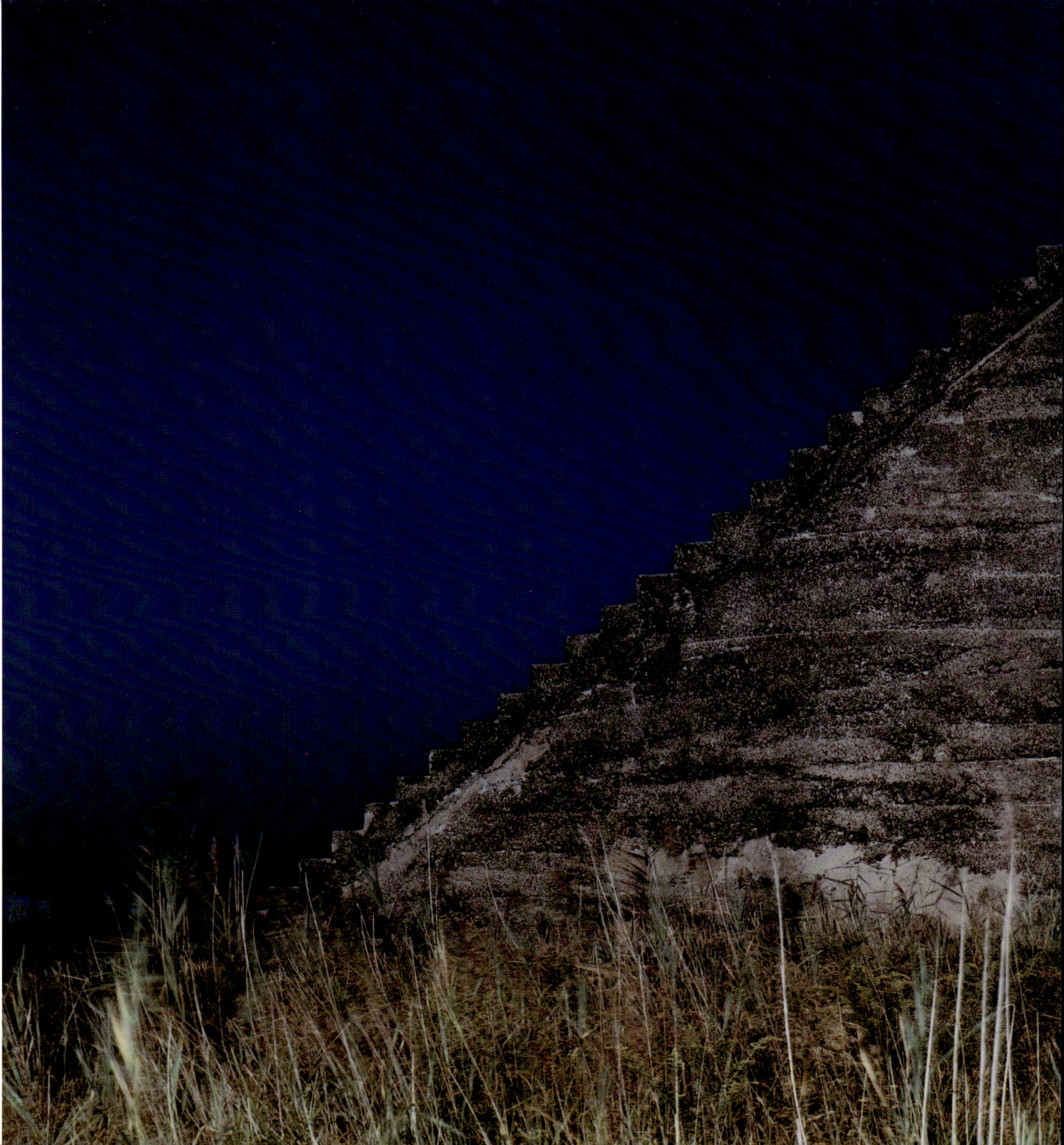

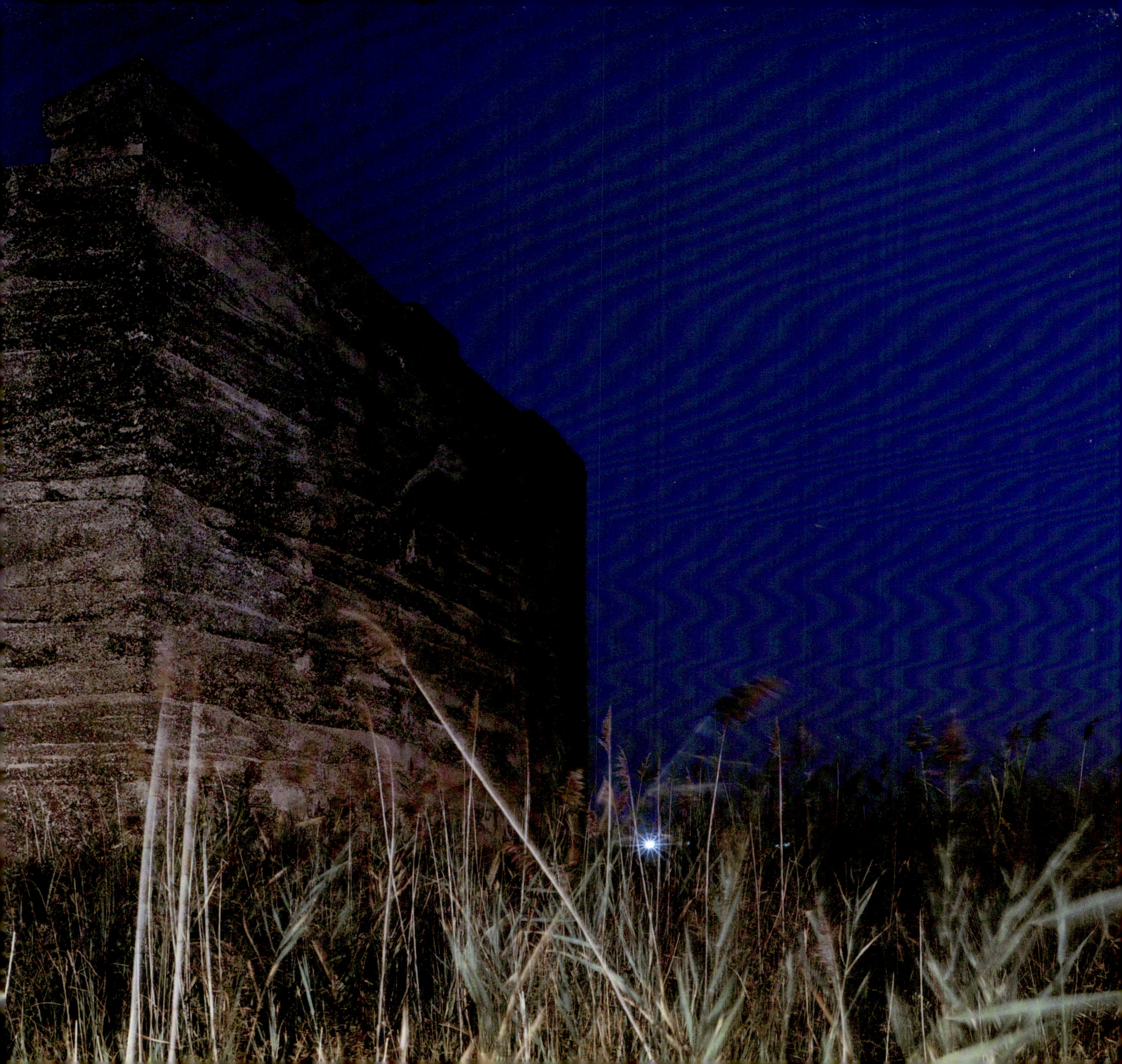

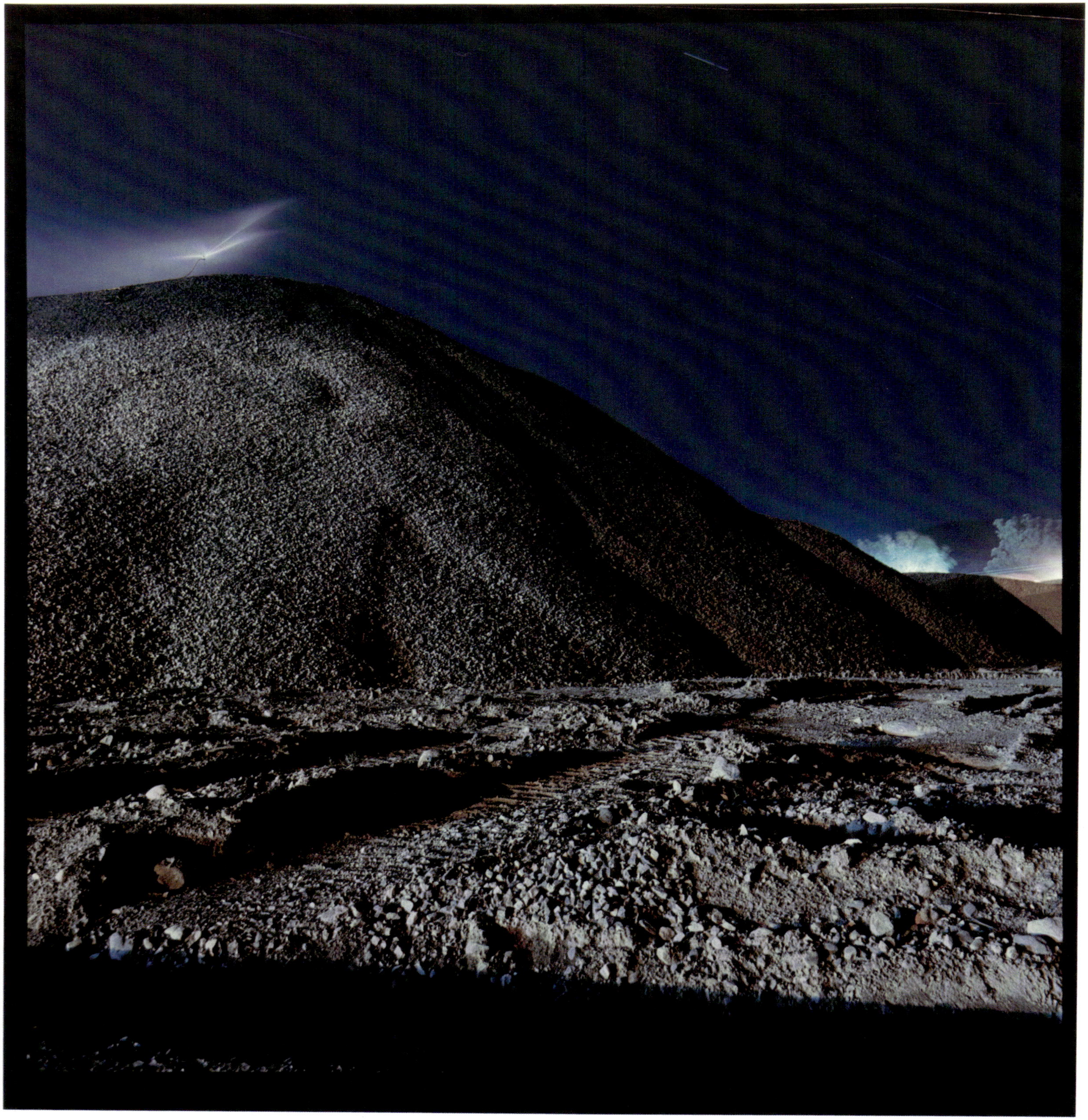

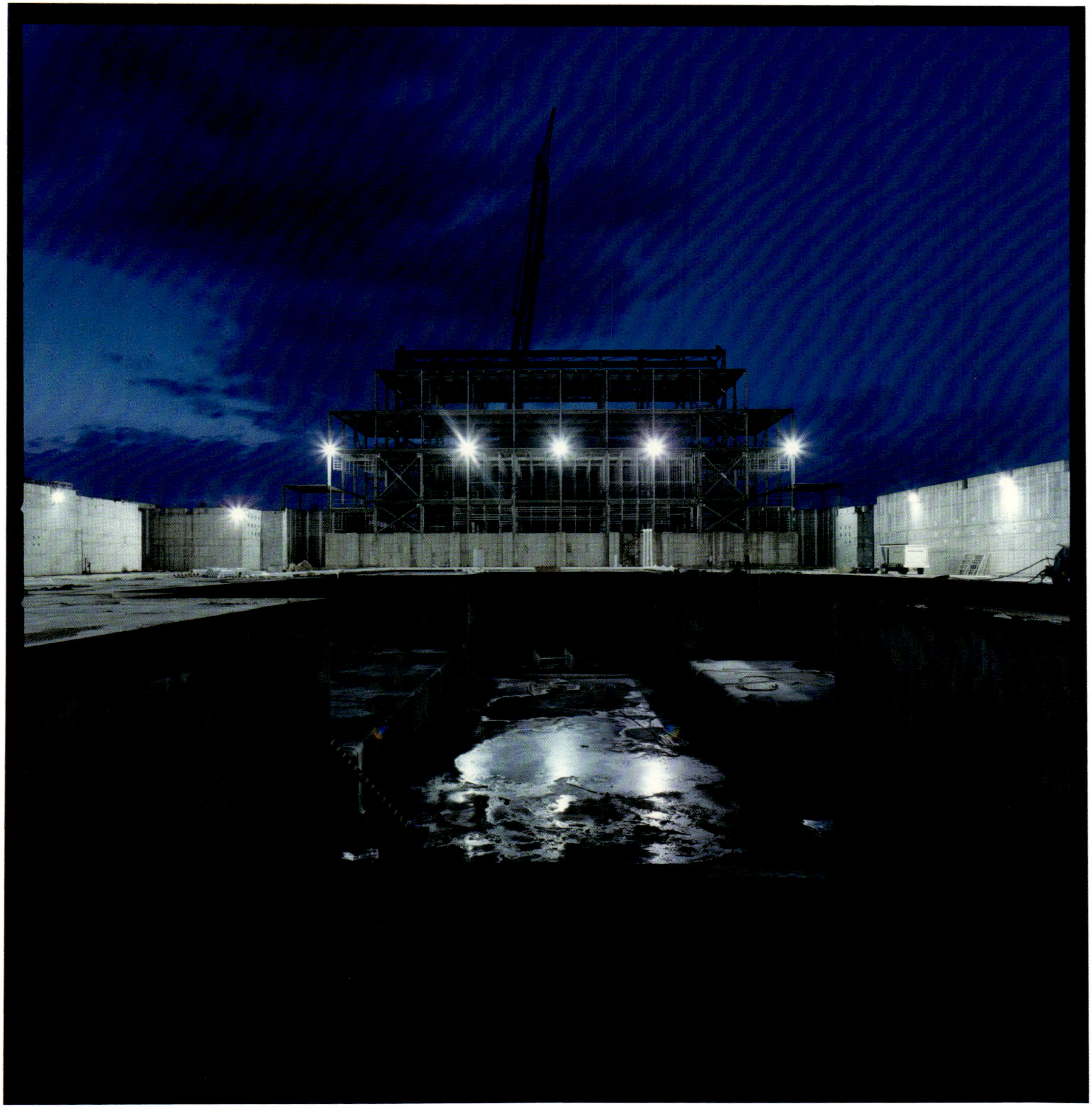

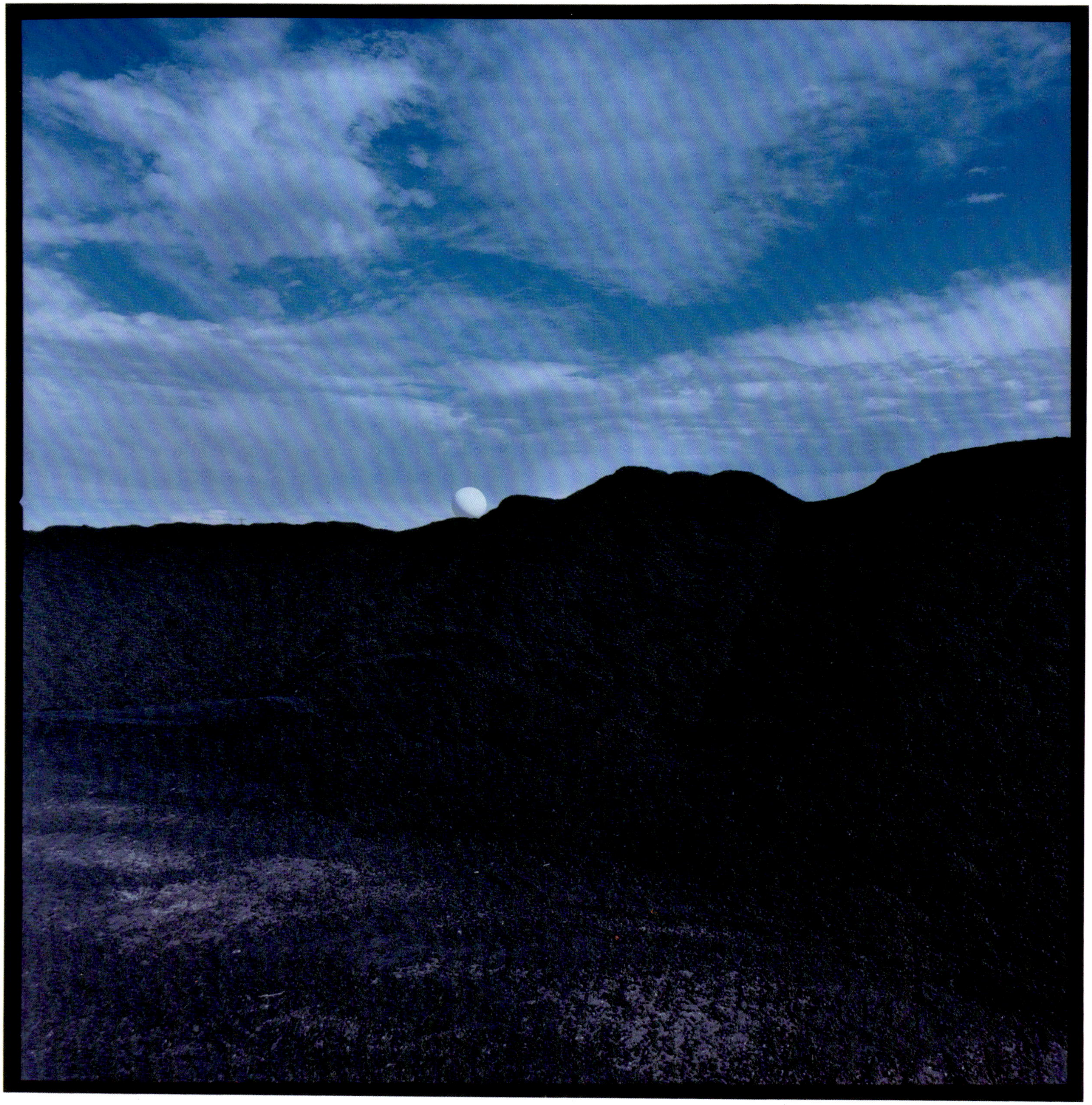

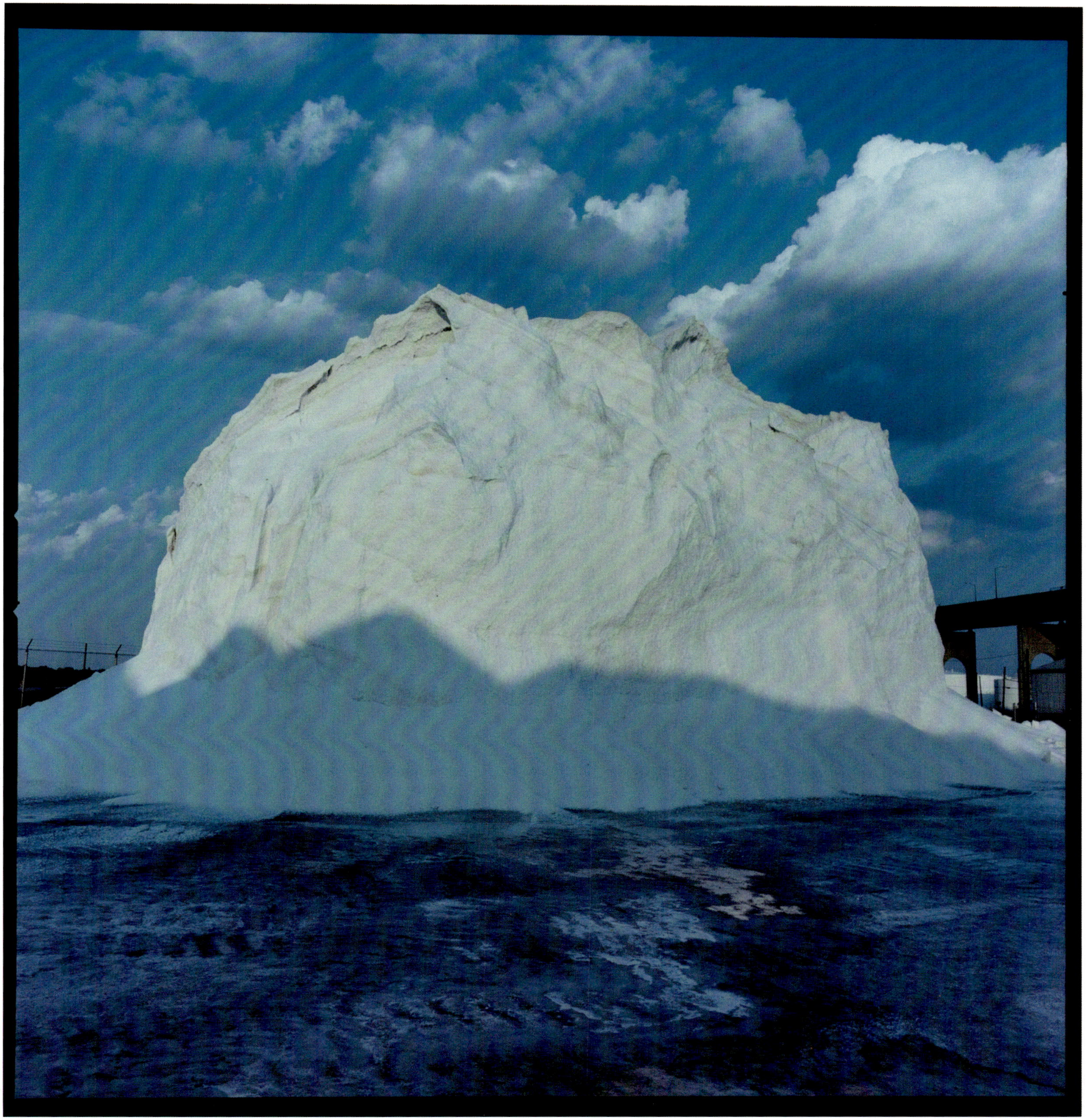

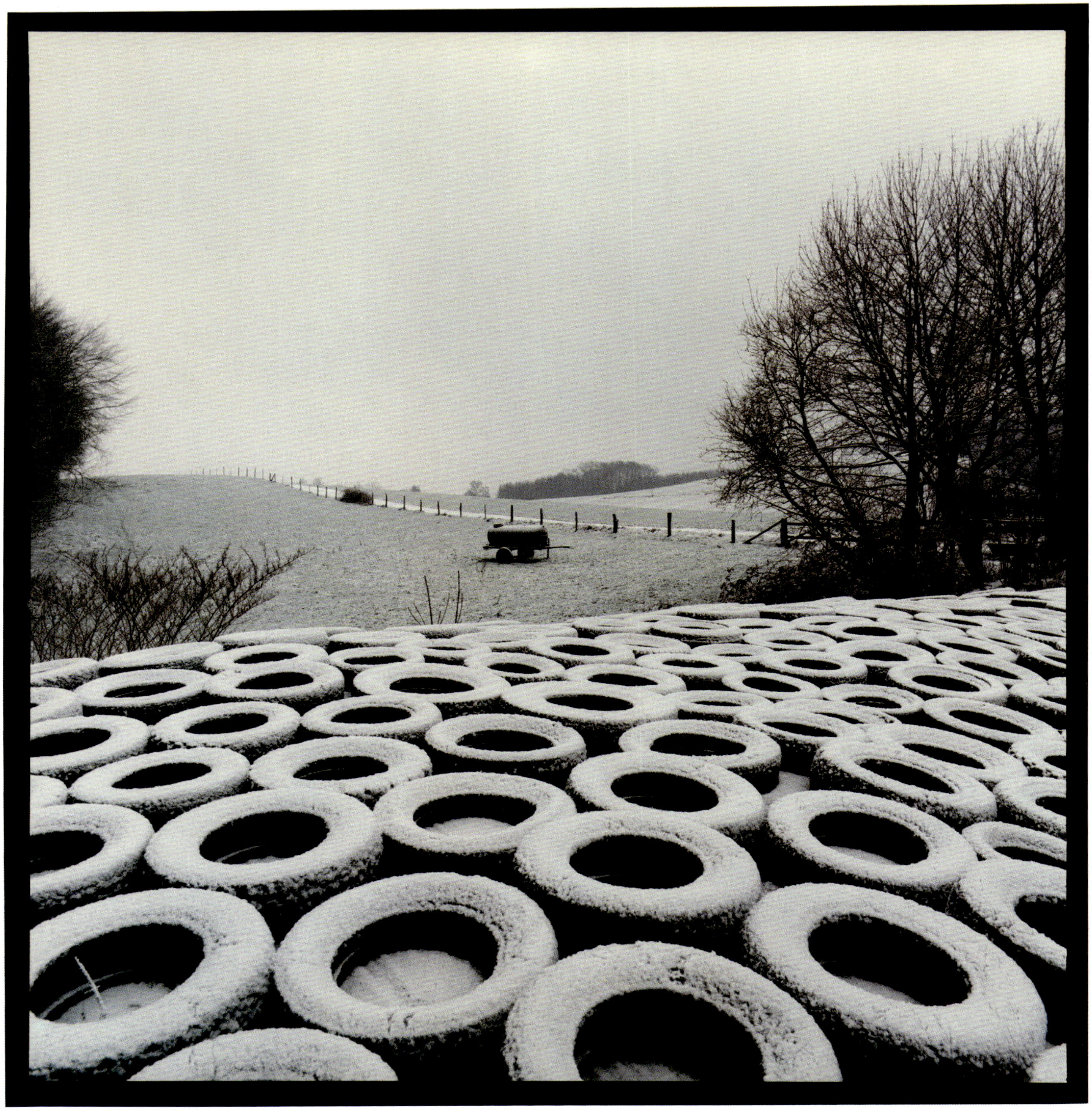

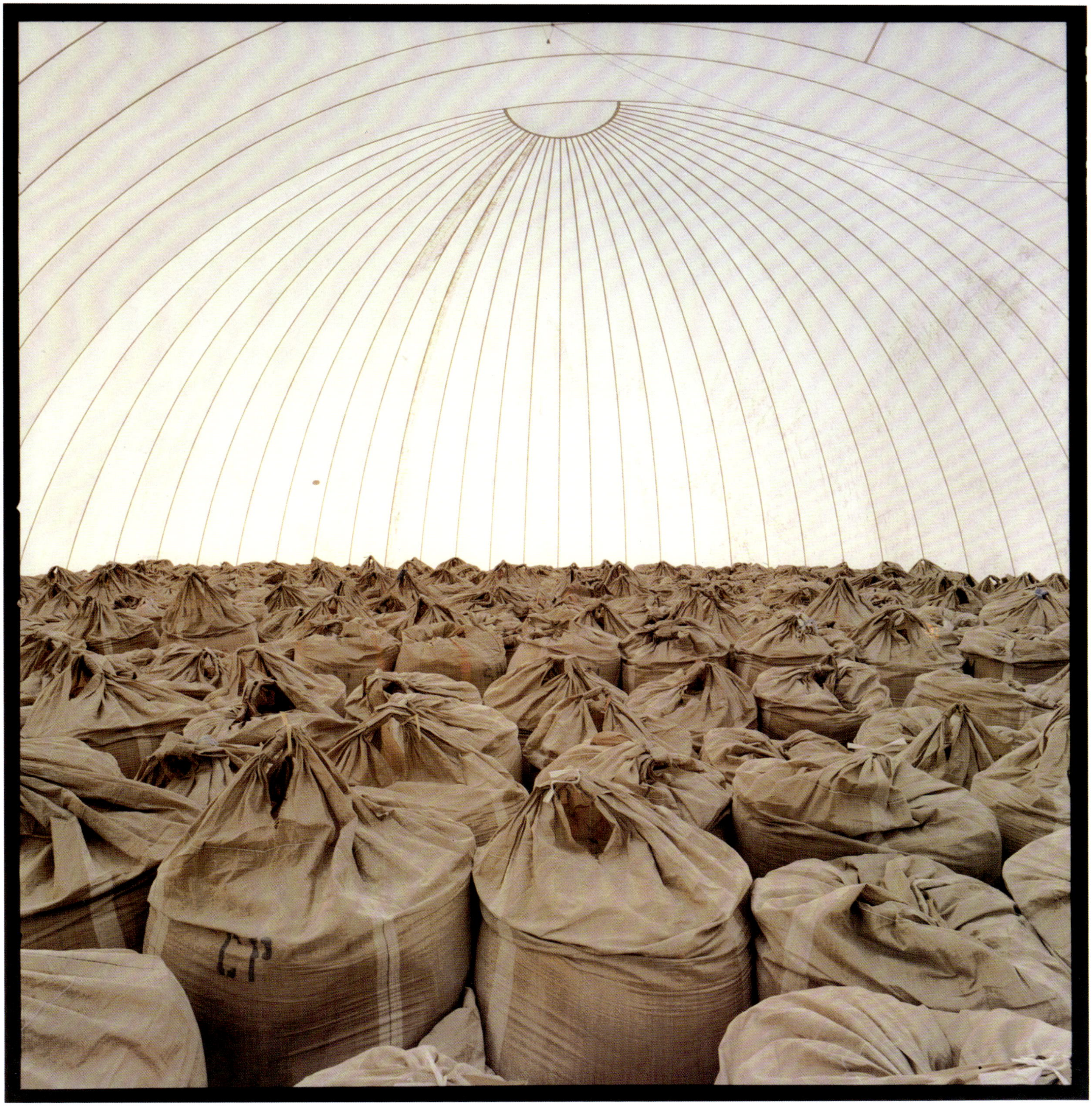
CP

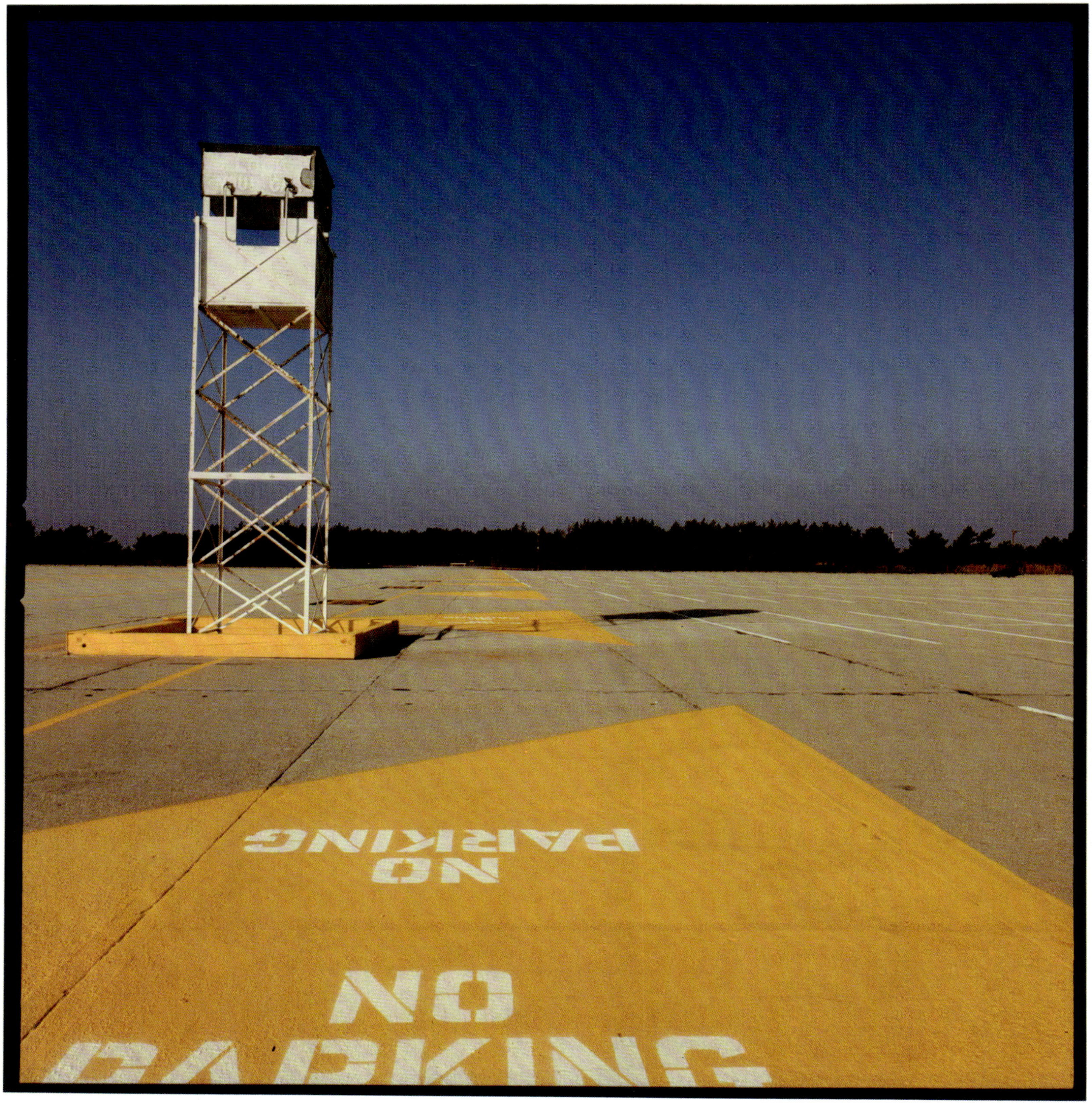
NO
PARKING
NO

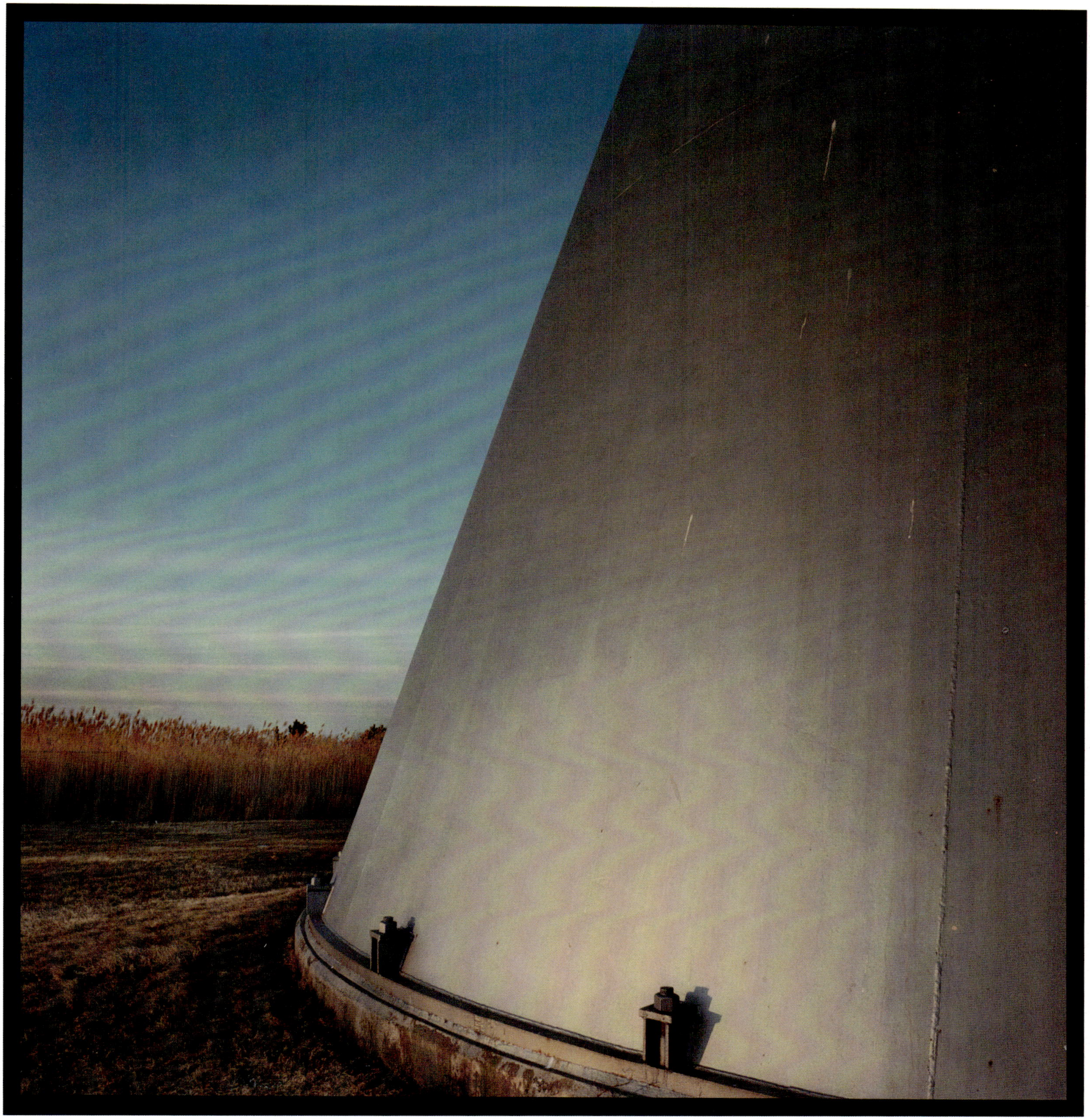

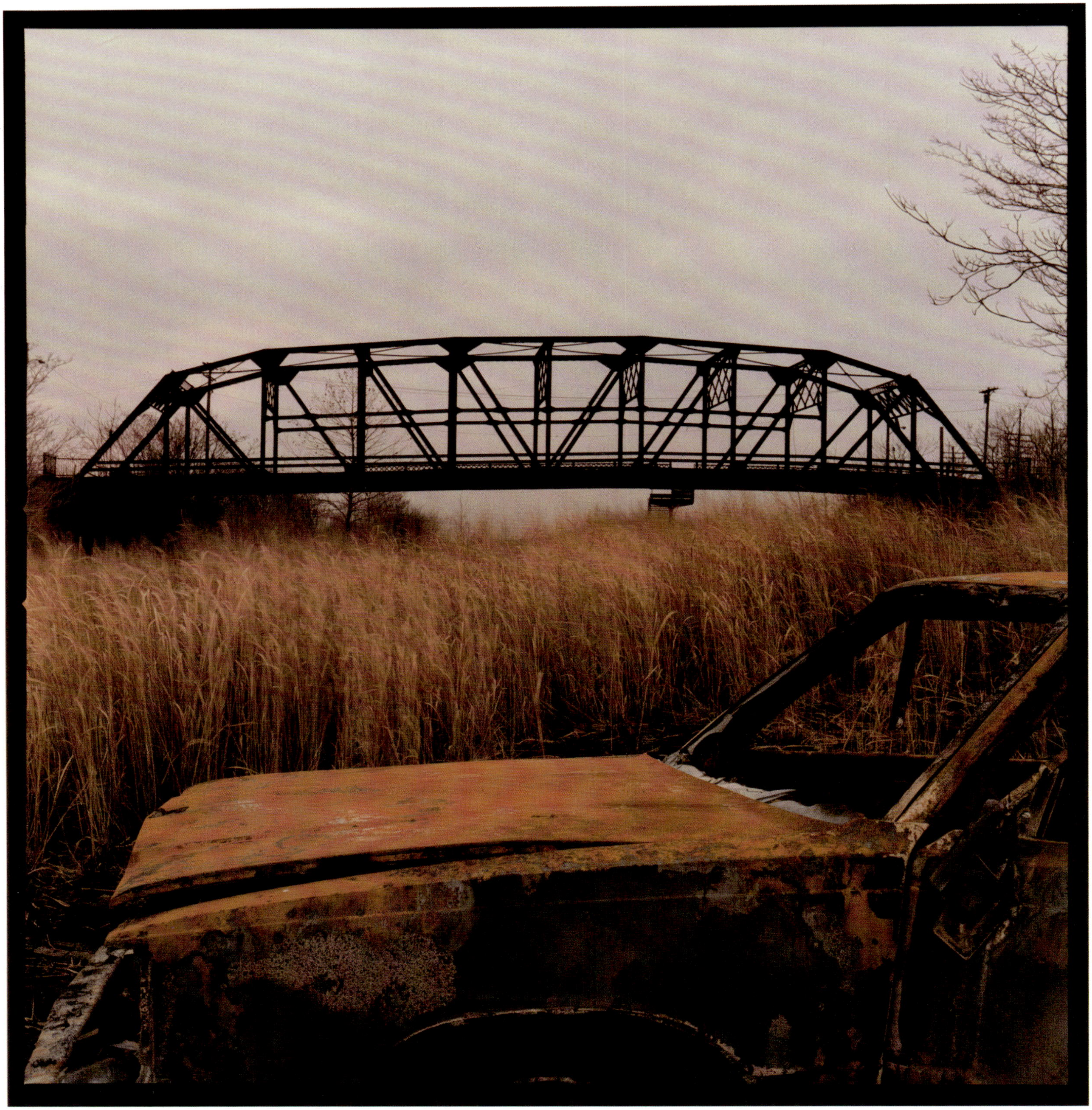

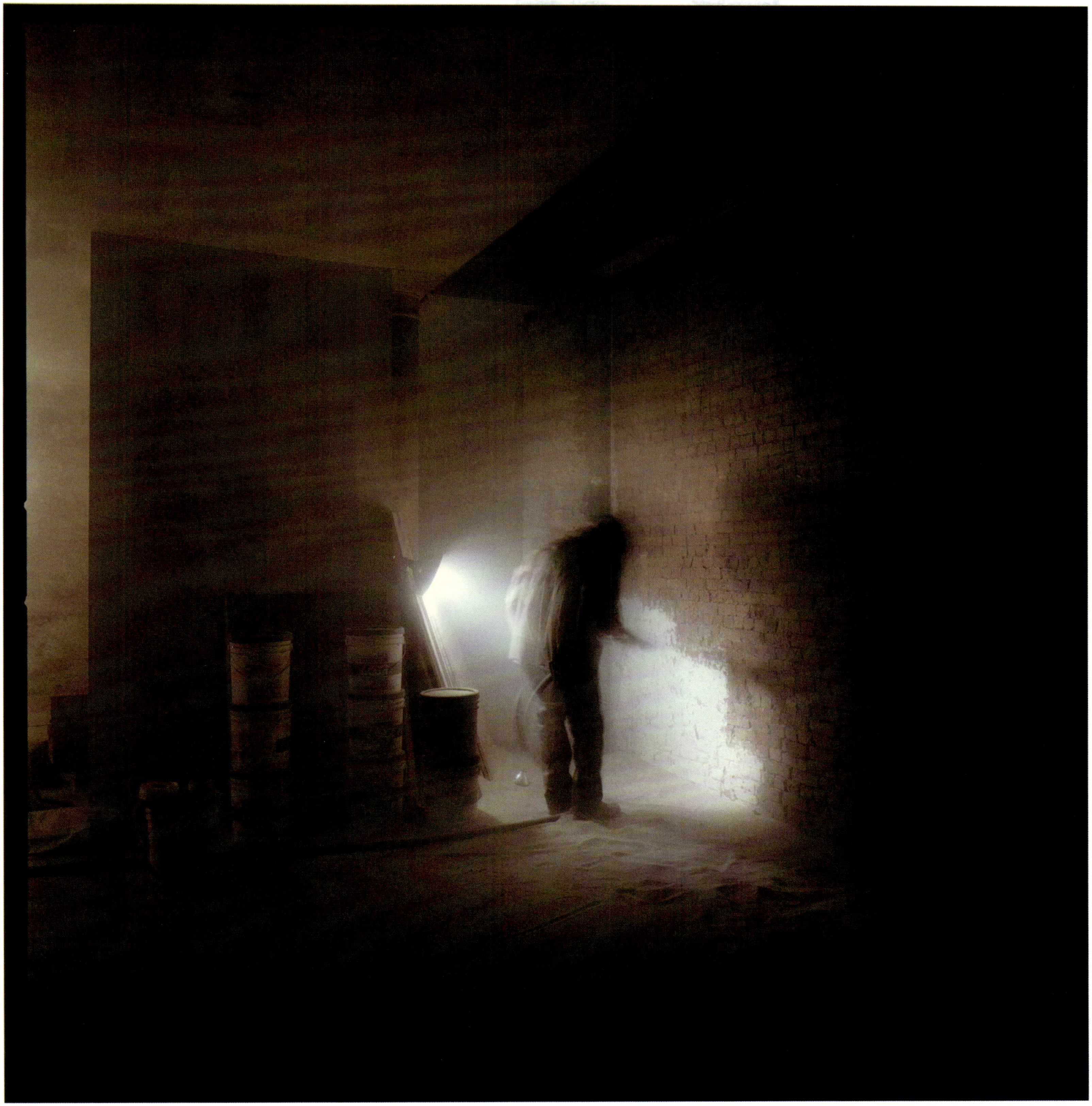

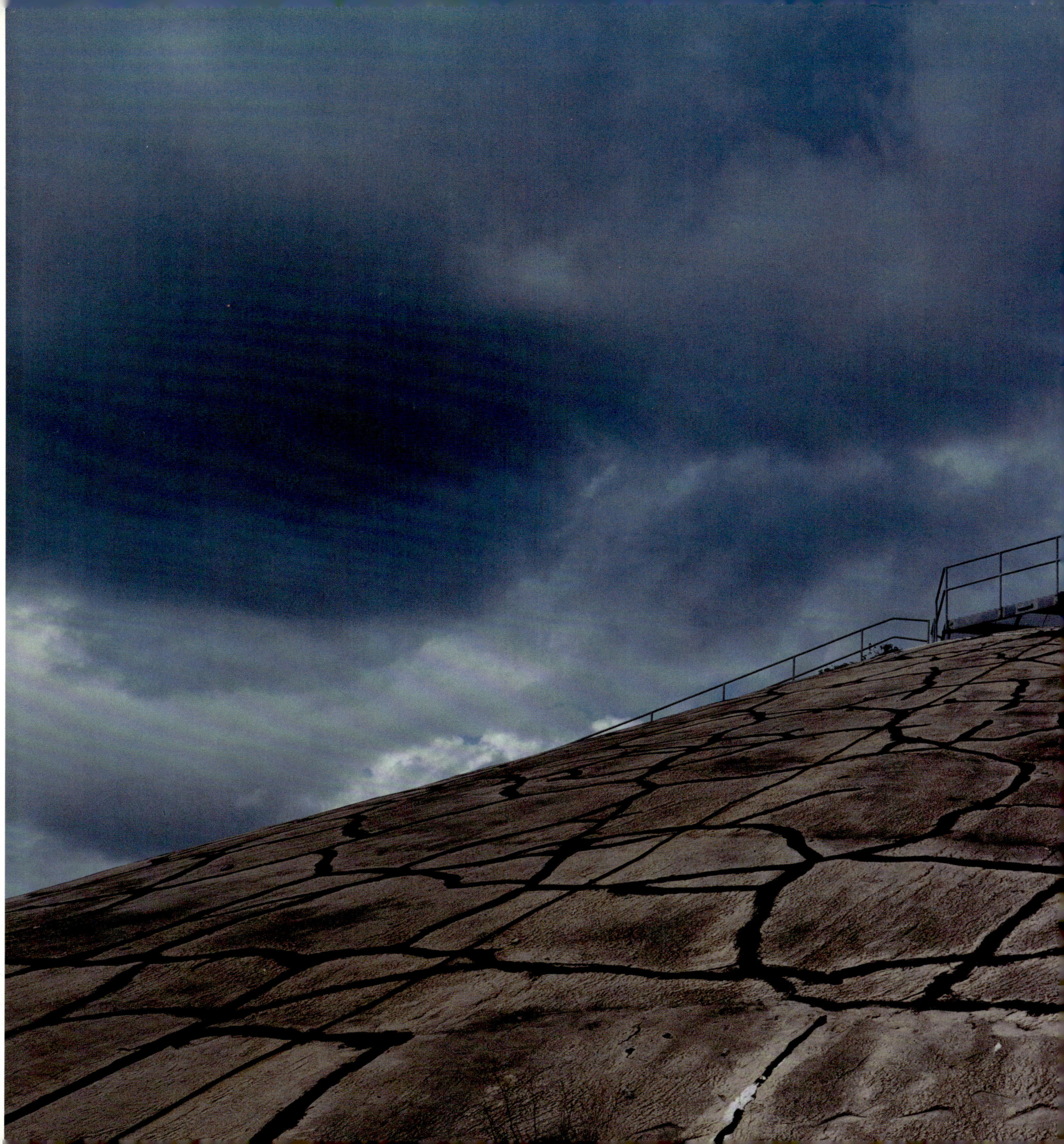

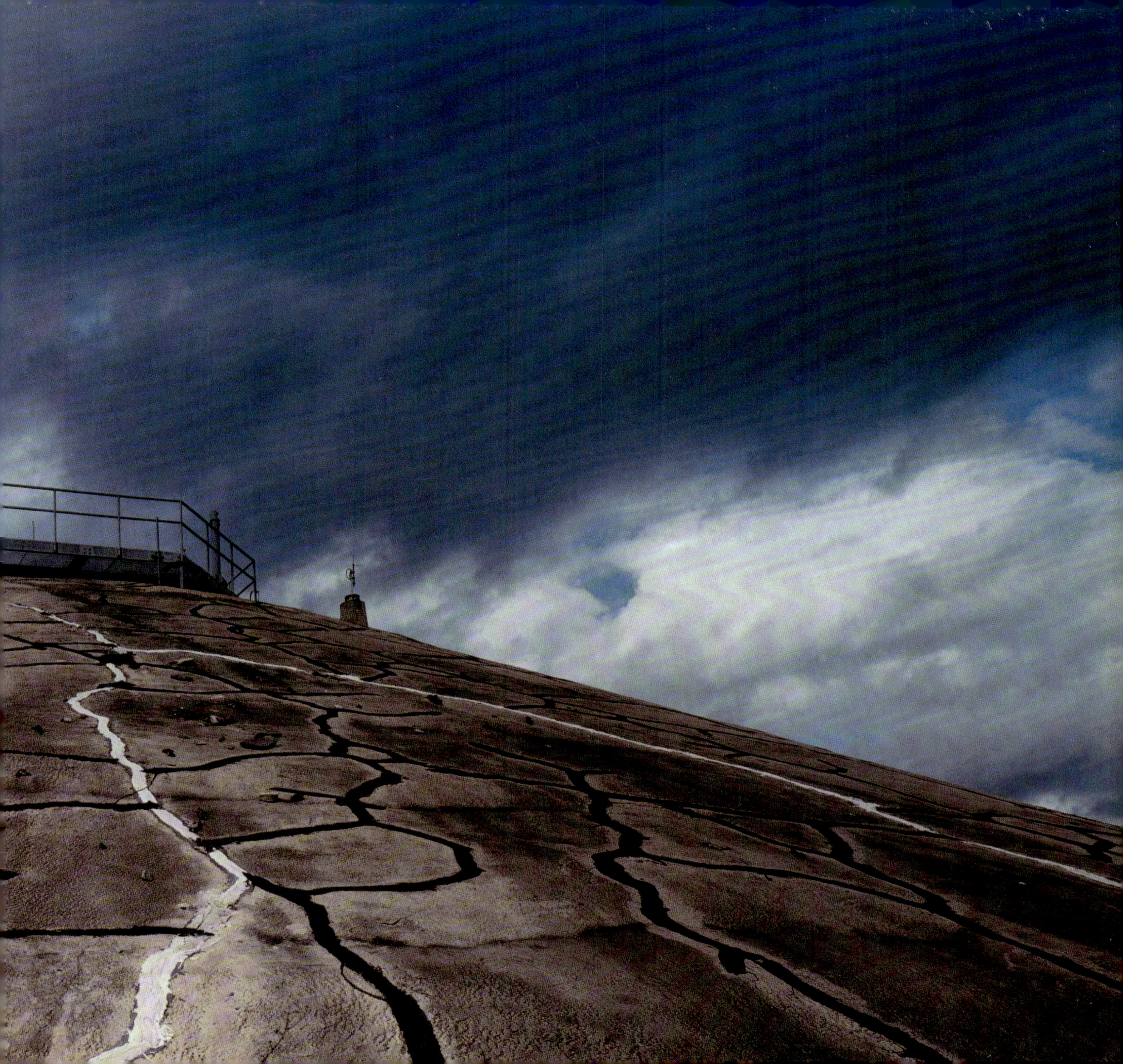

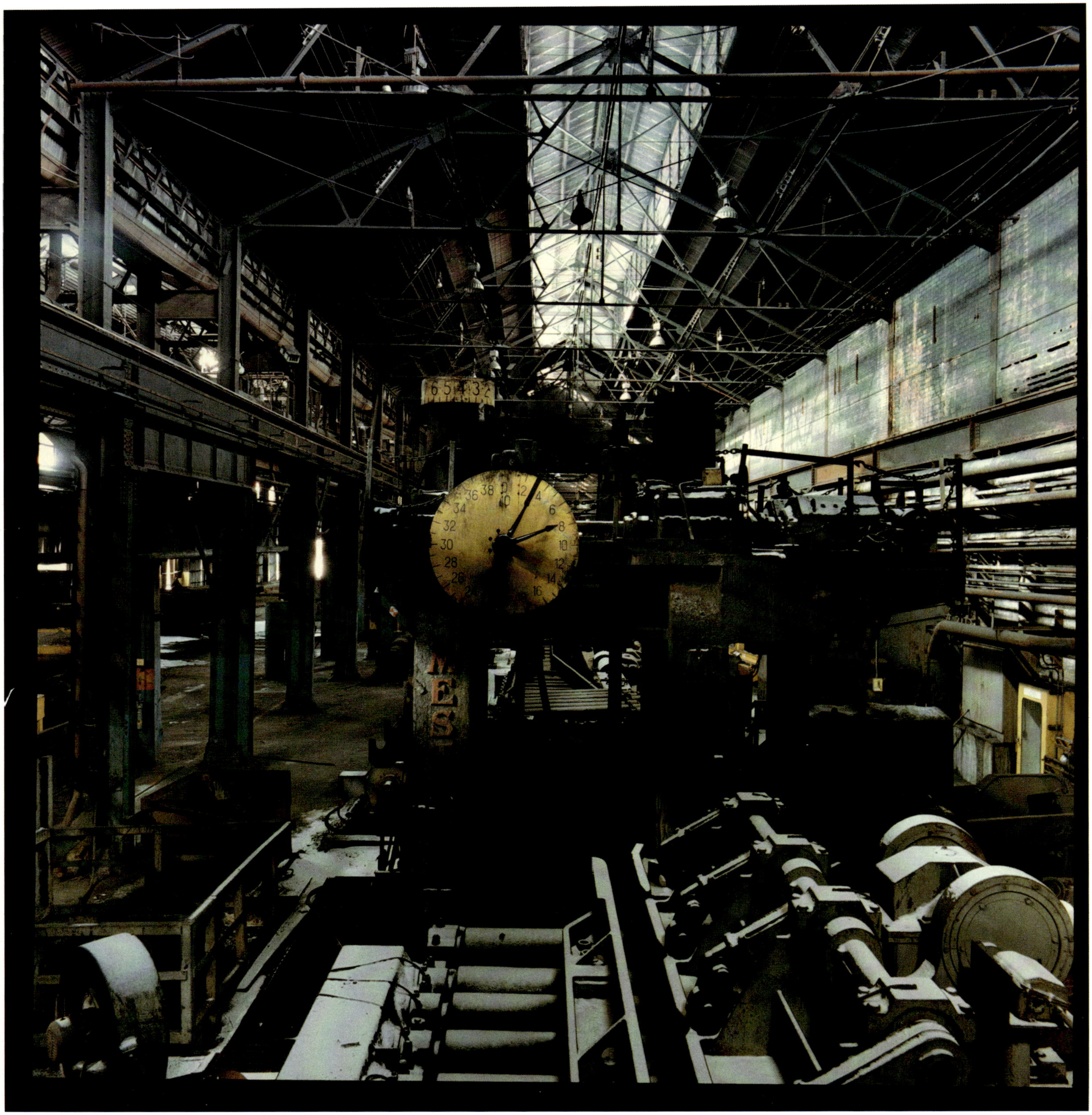

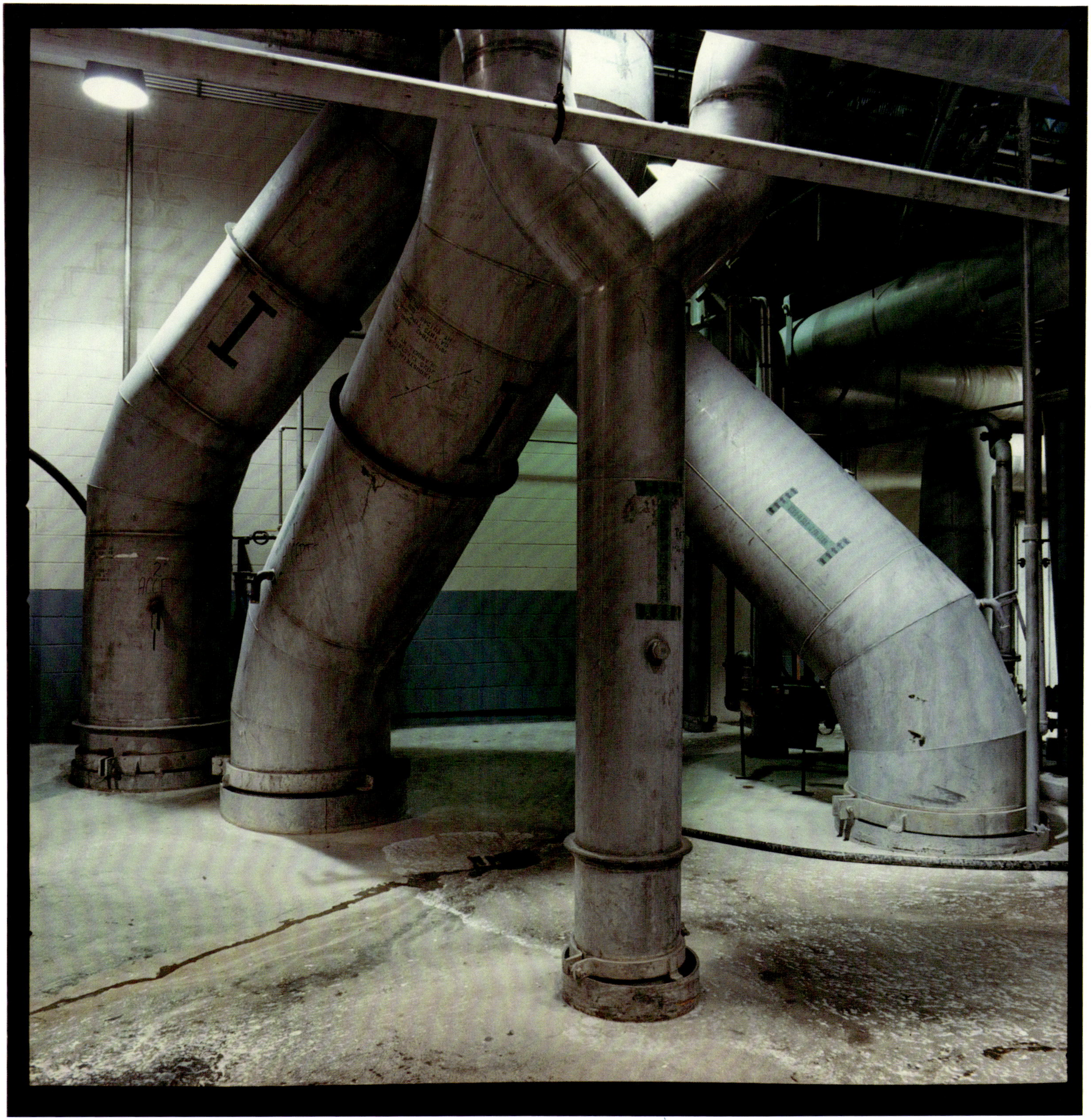

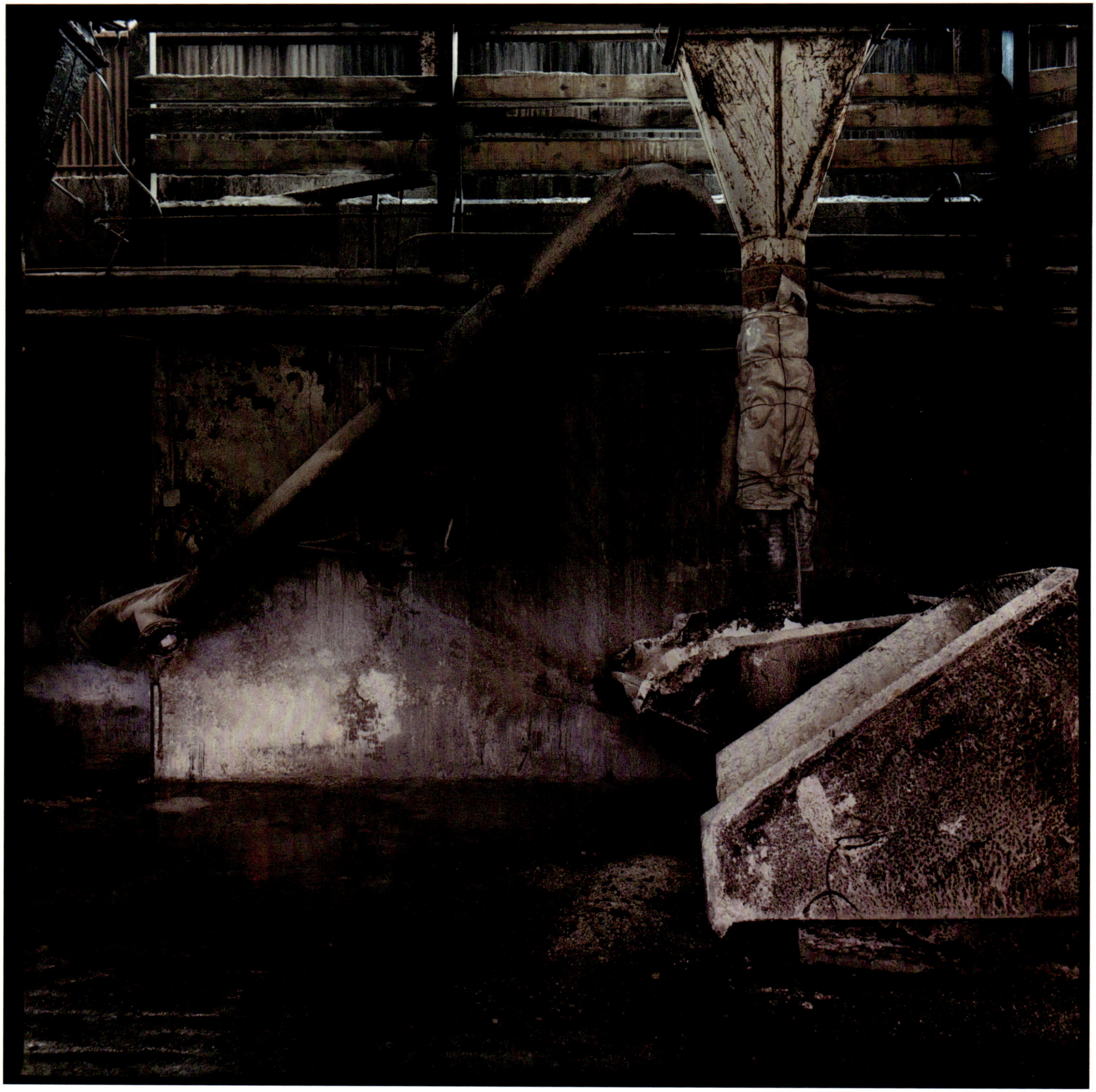

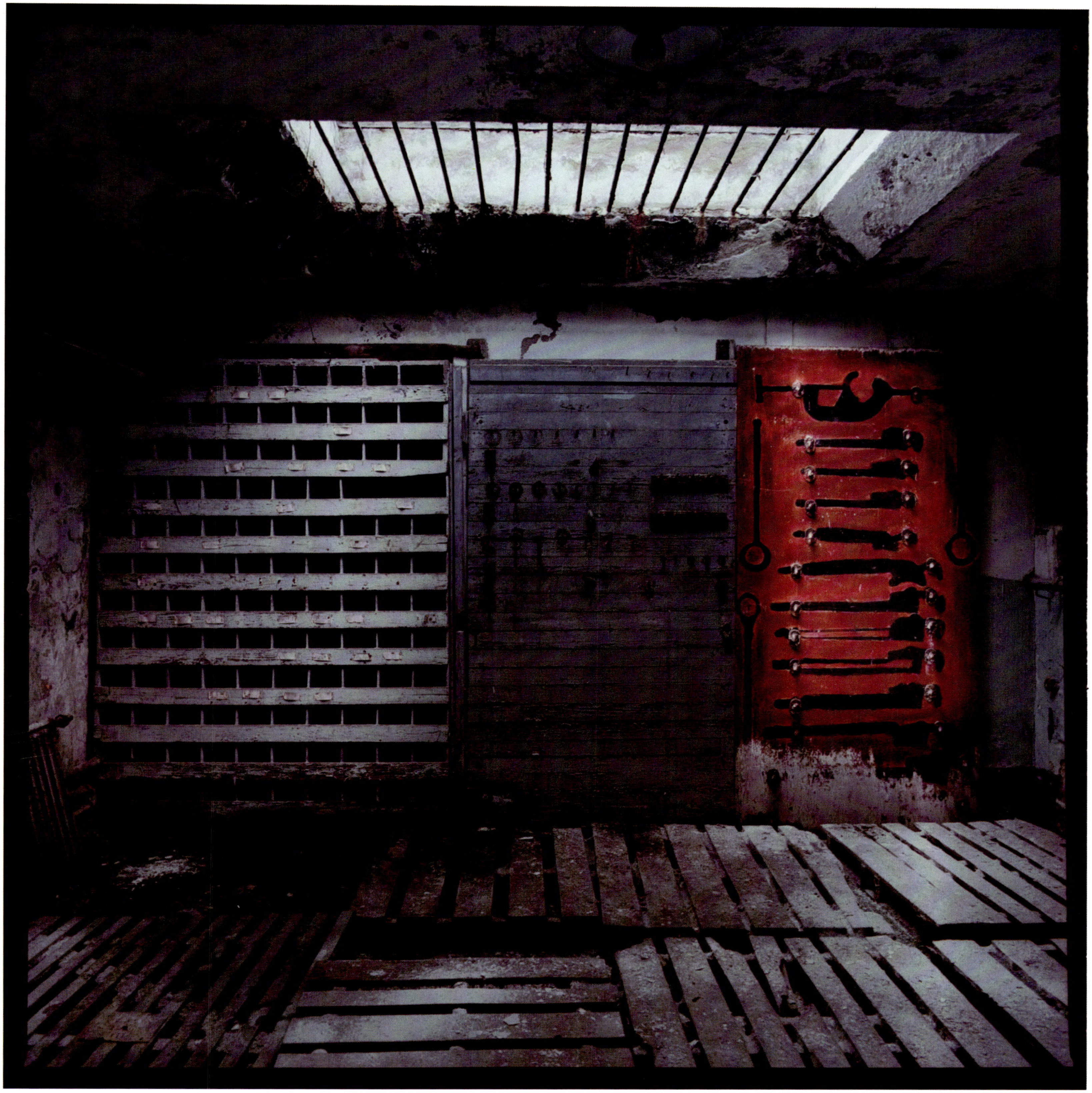

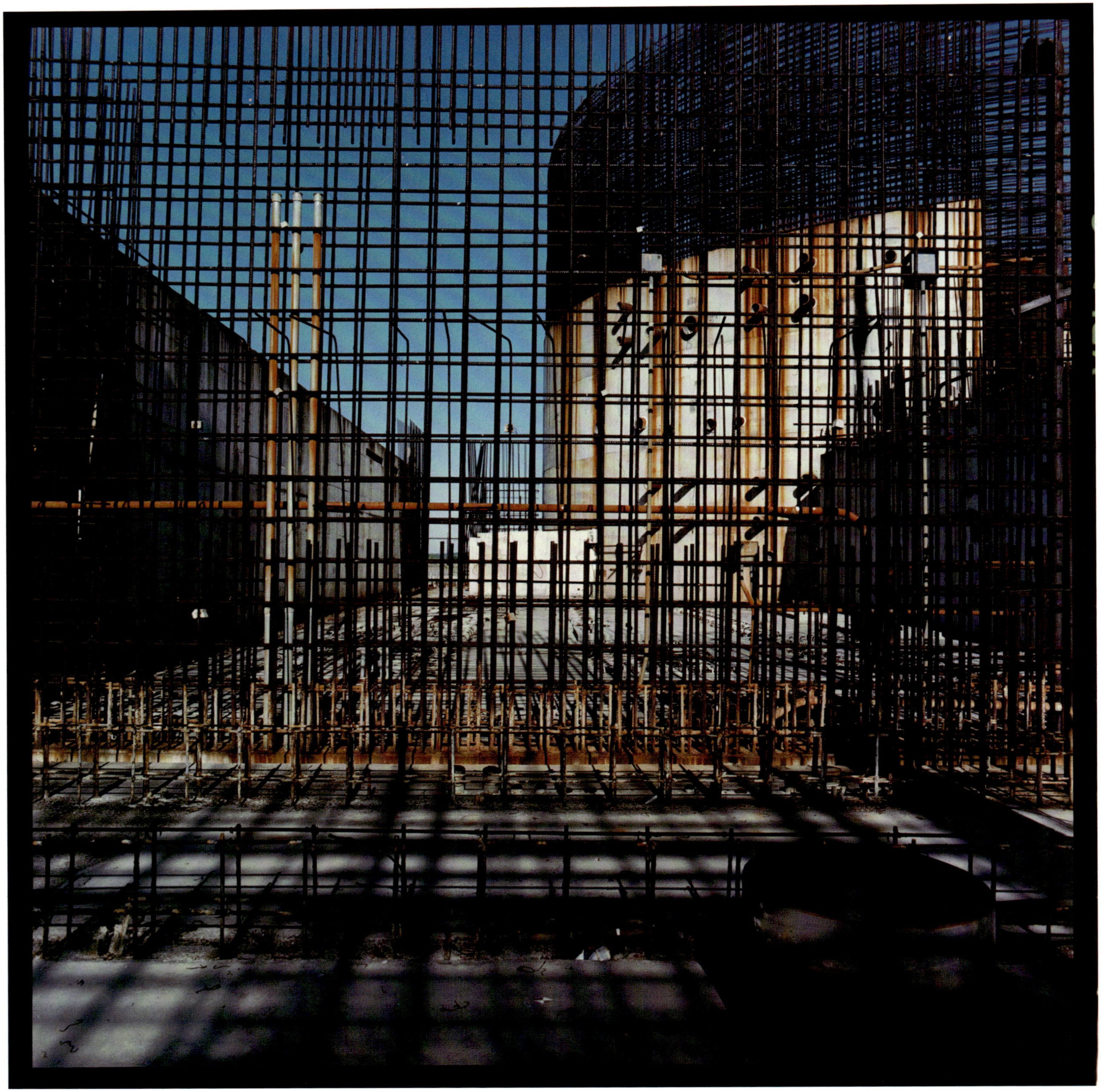

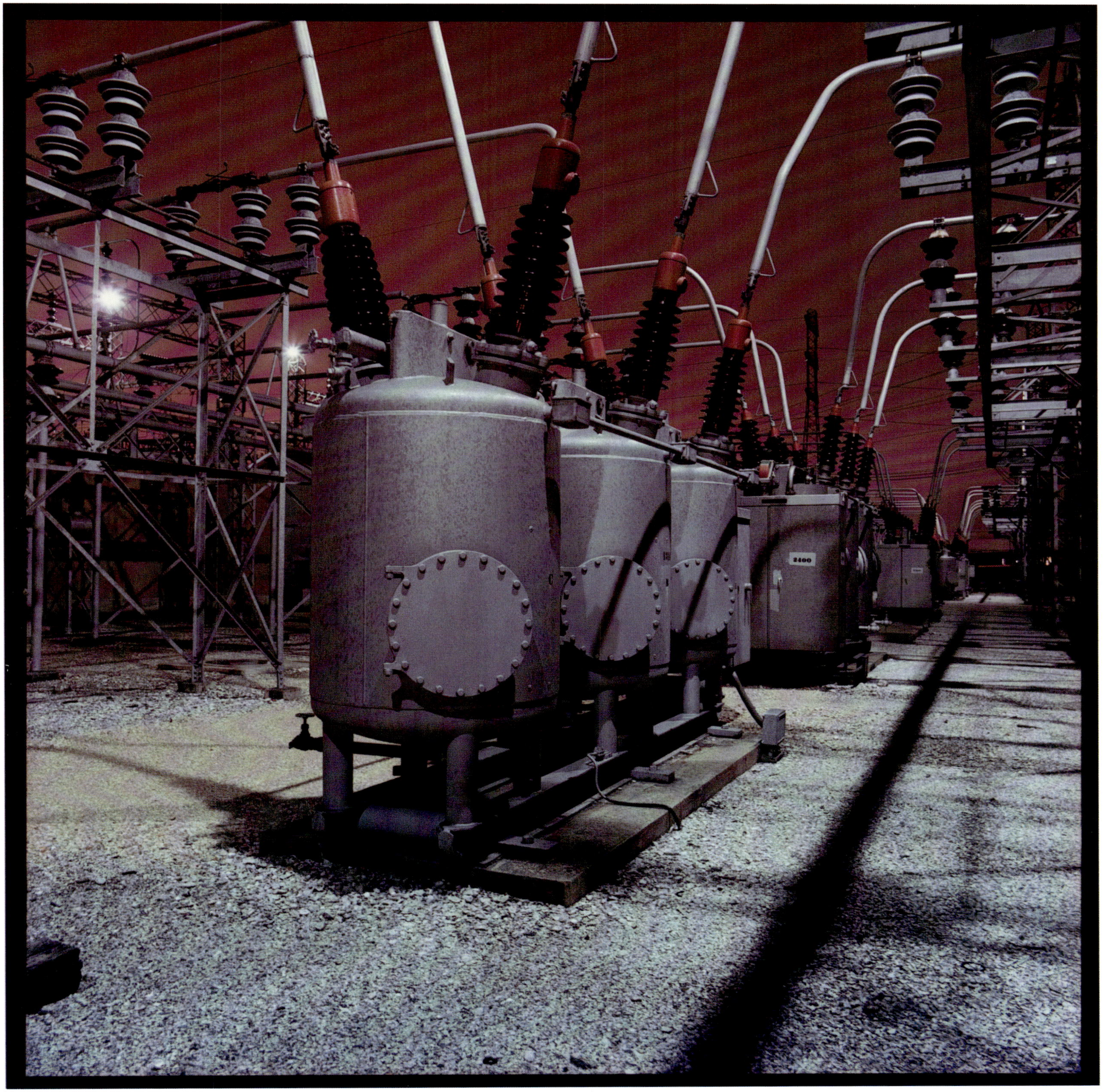
2400

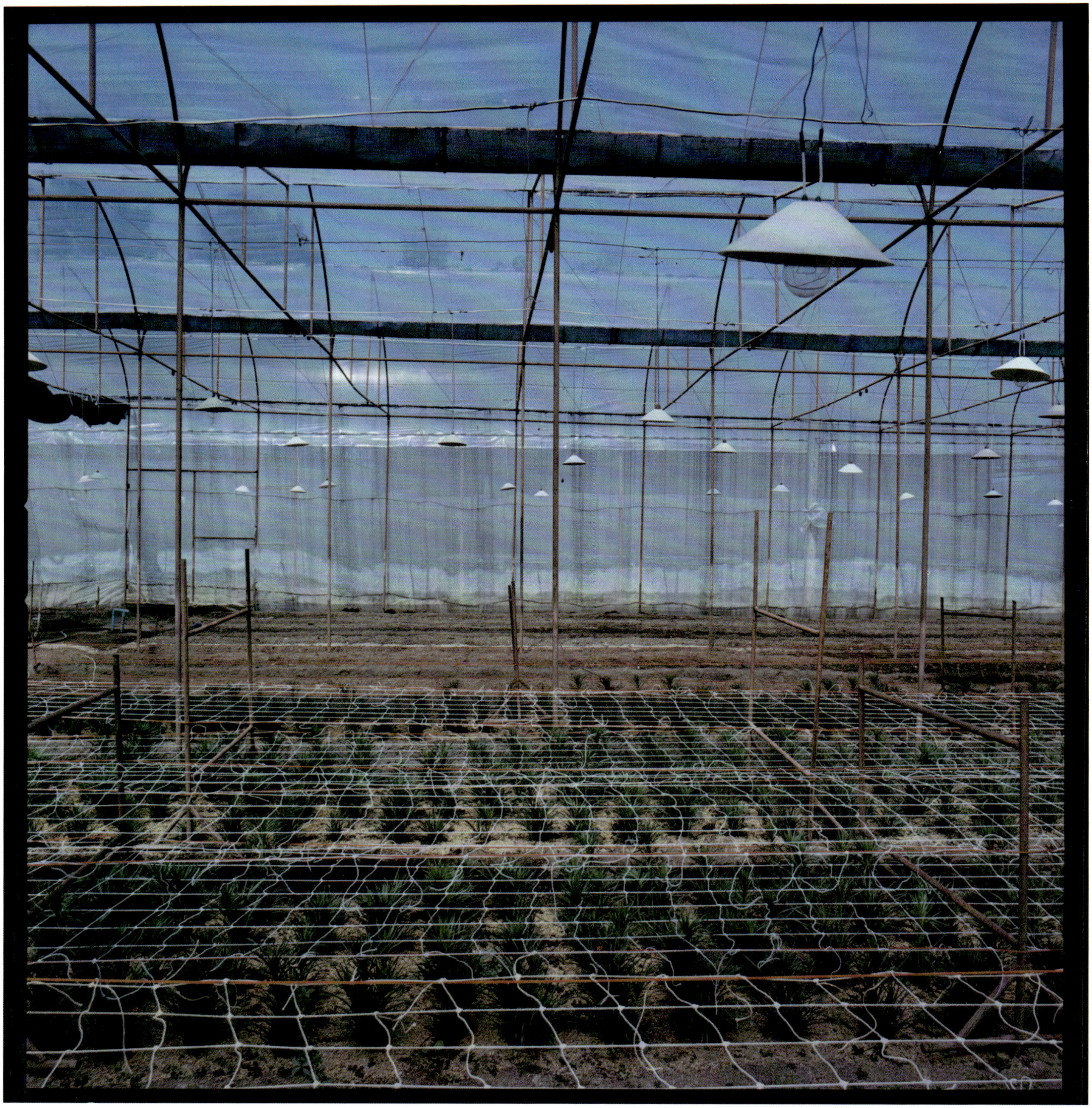

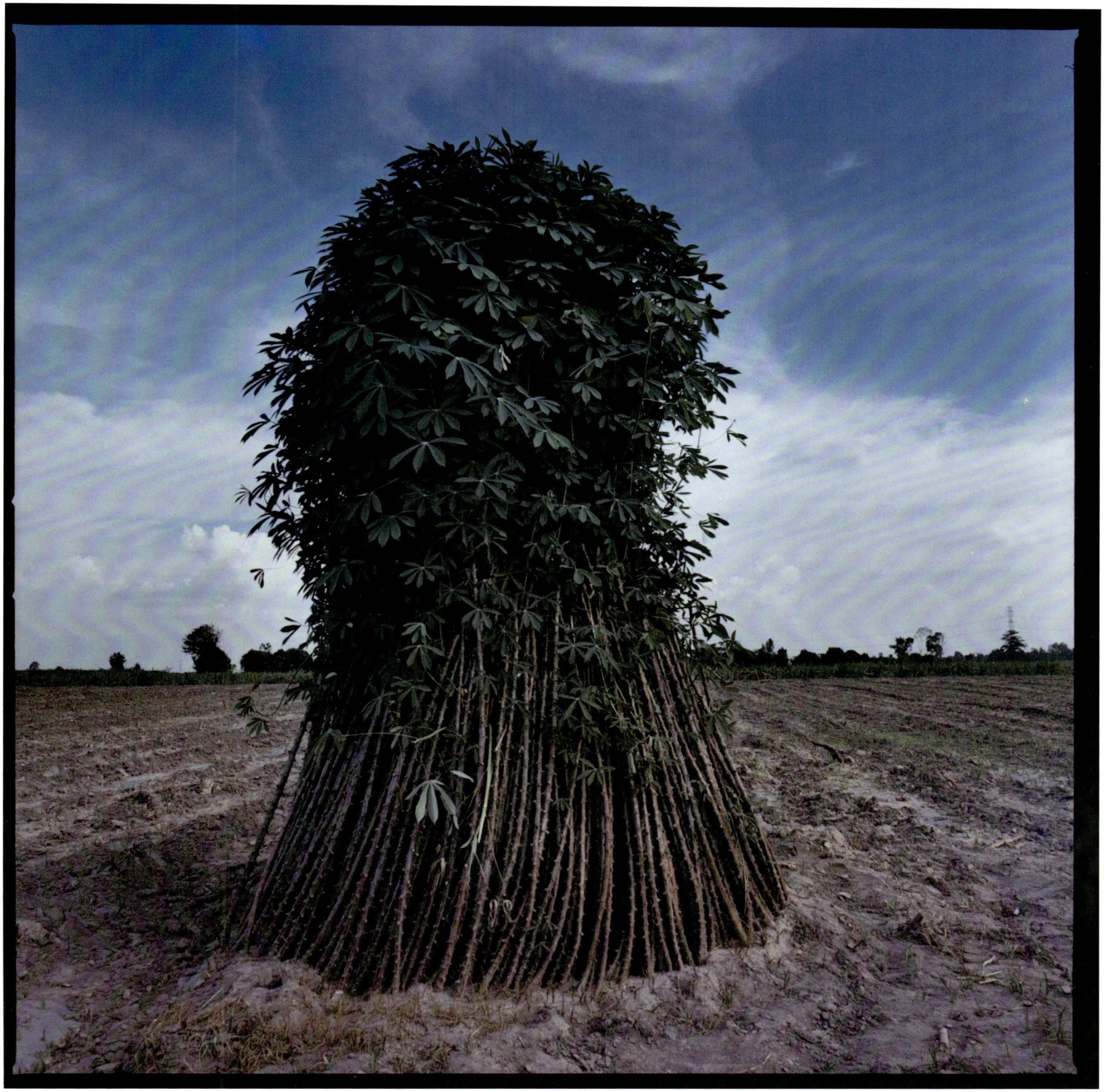

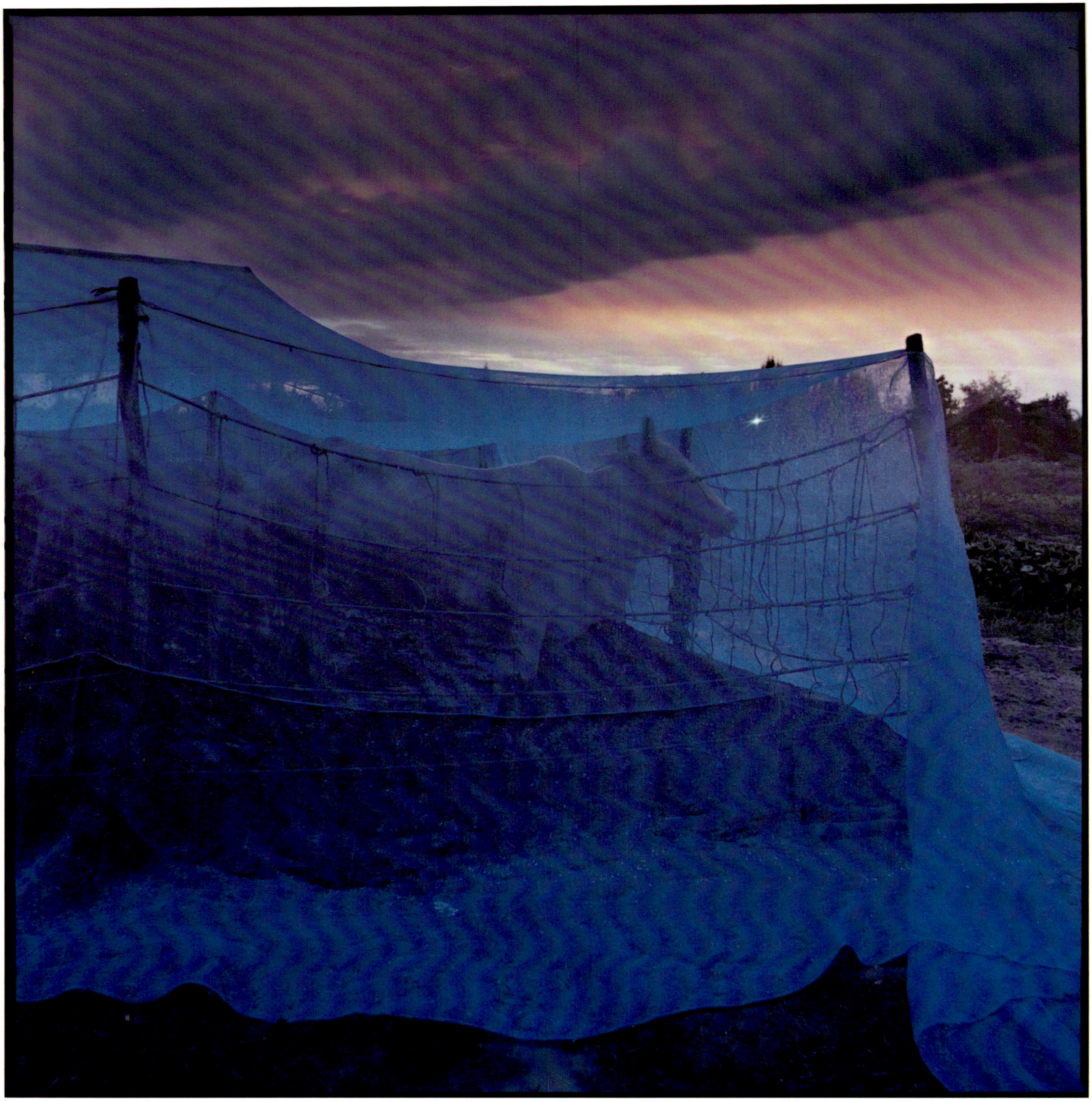

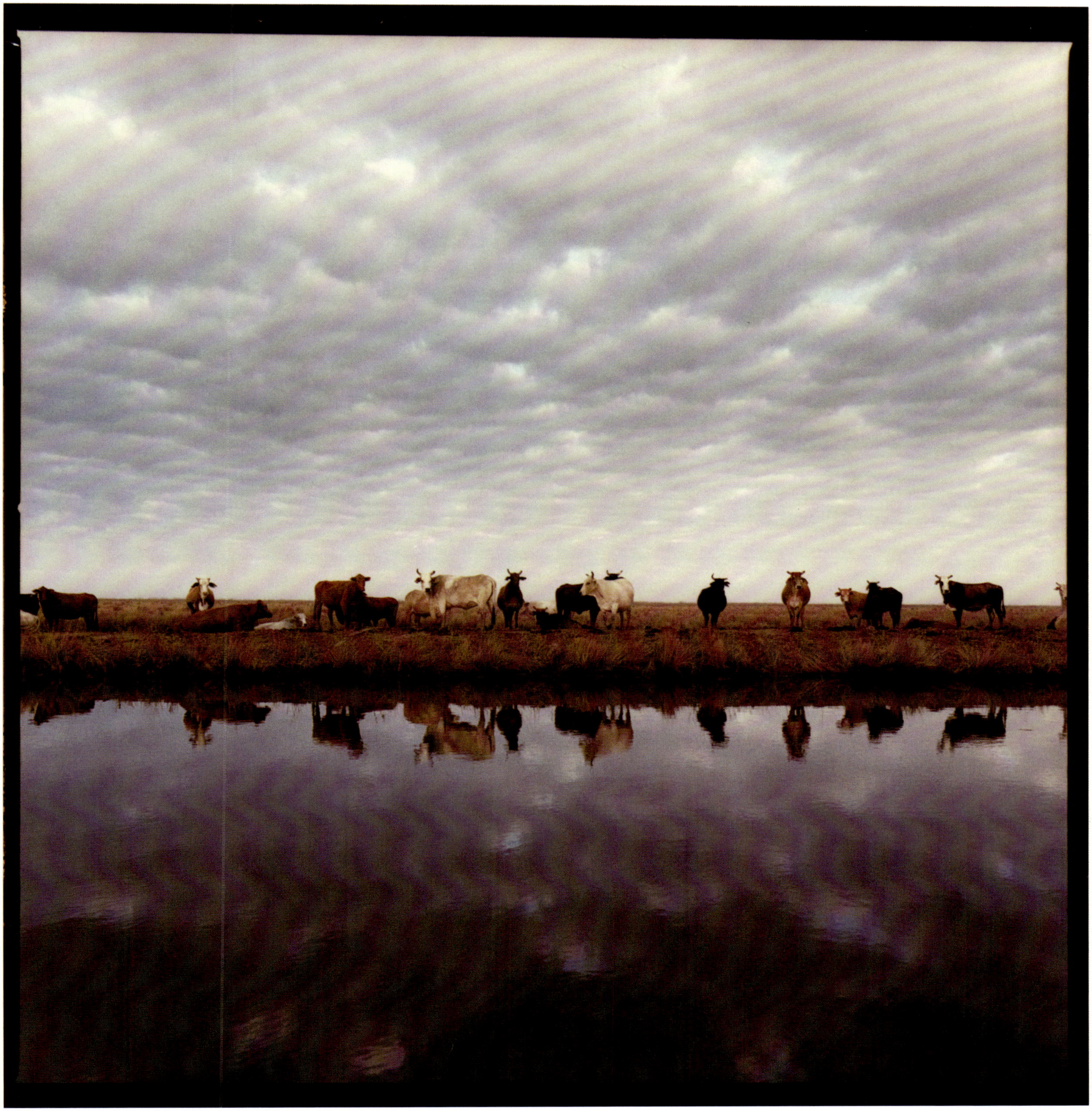

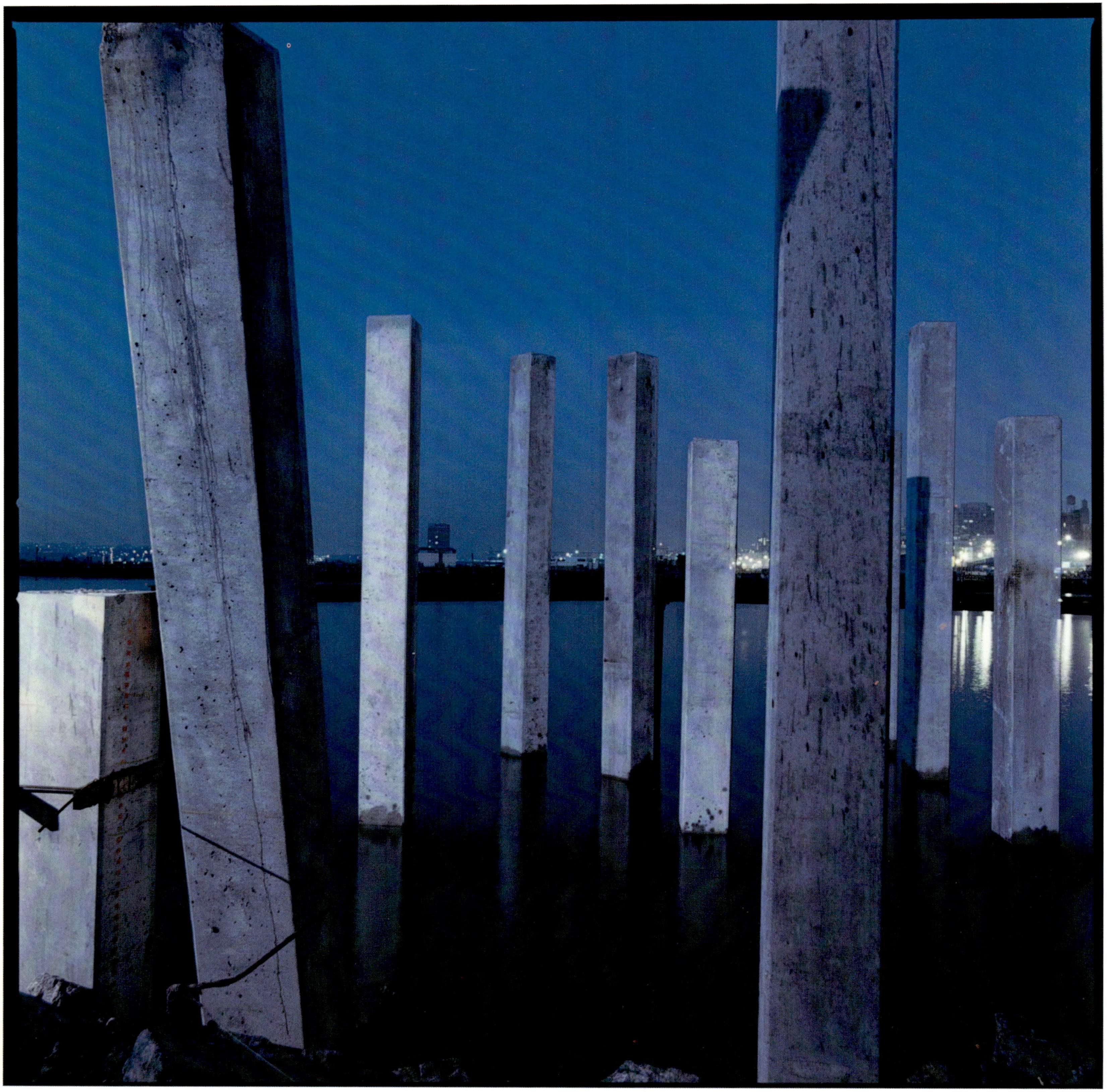

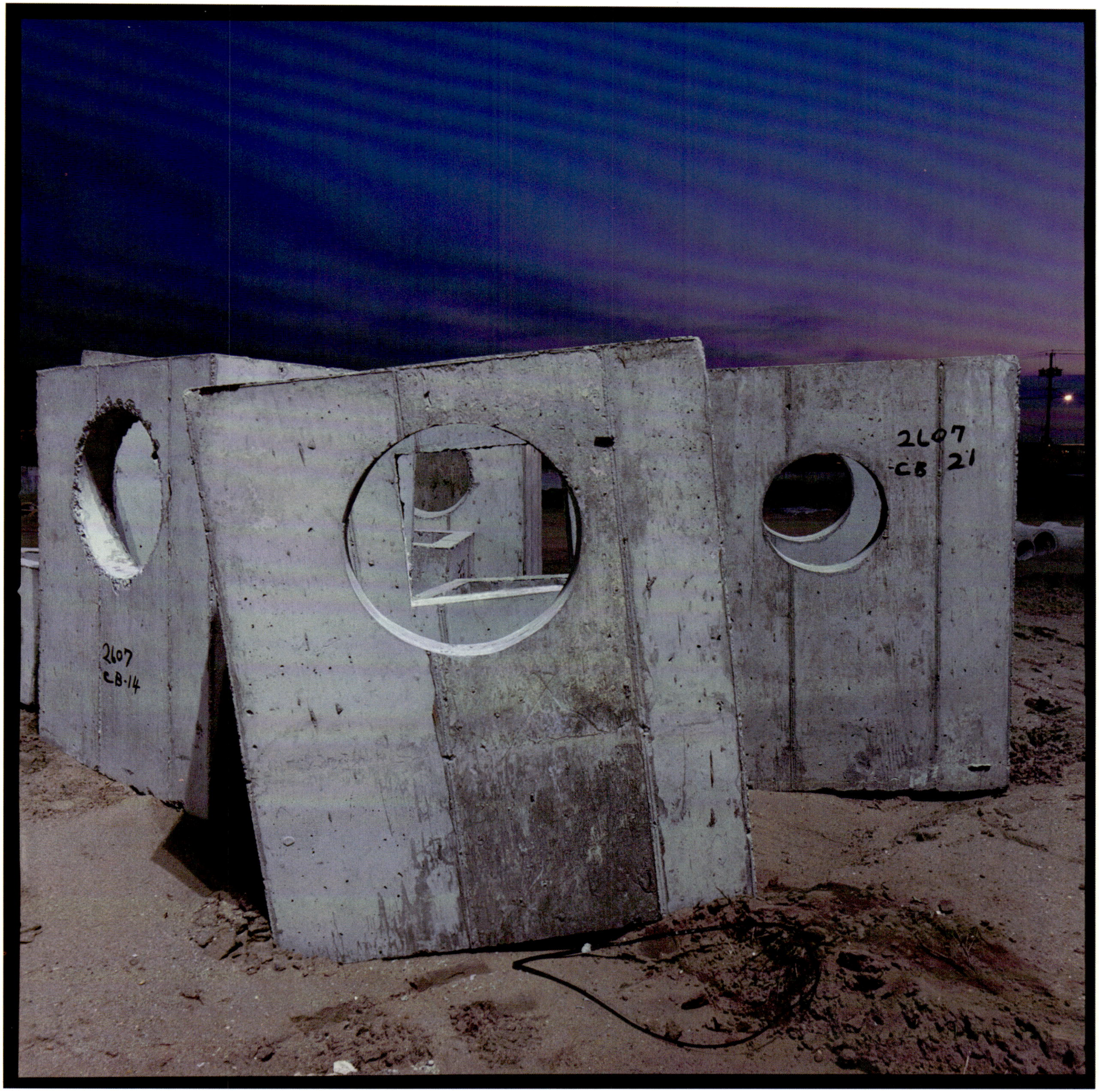
2607
CB 21
2607
CB-14

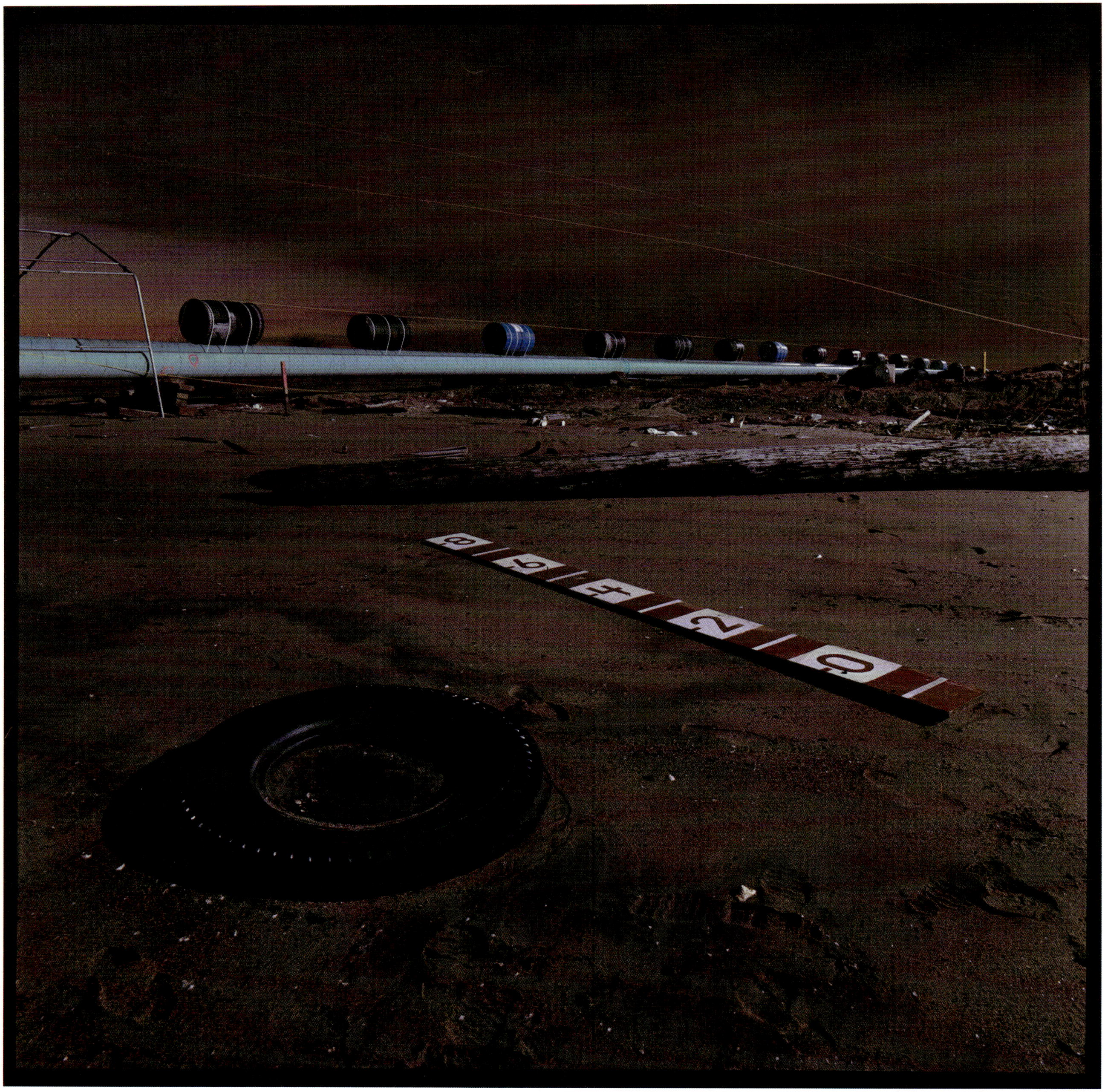

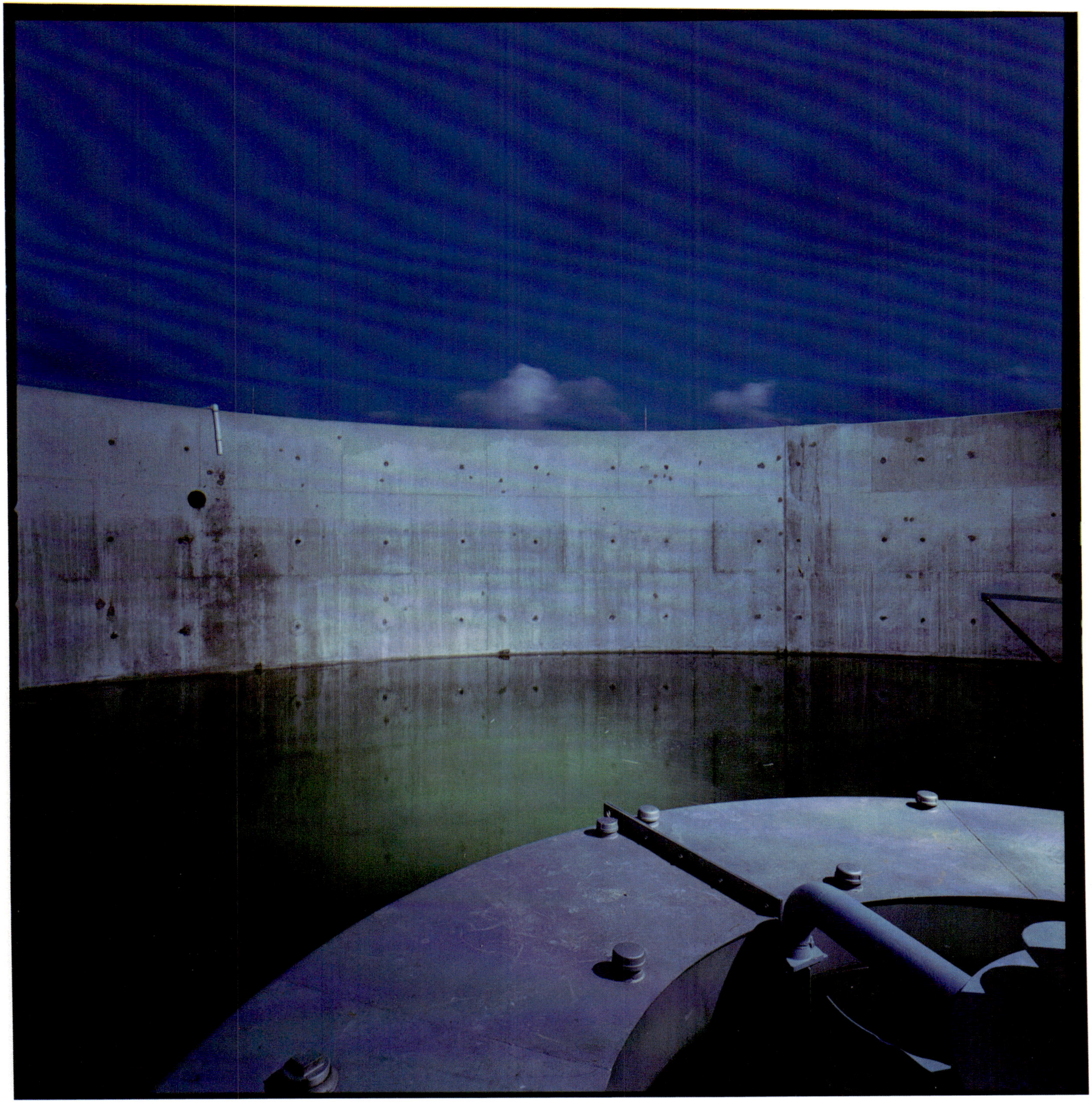

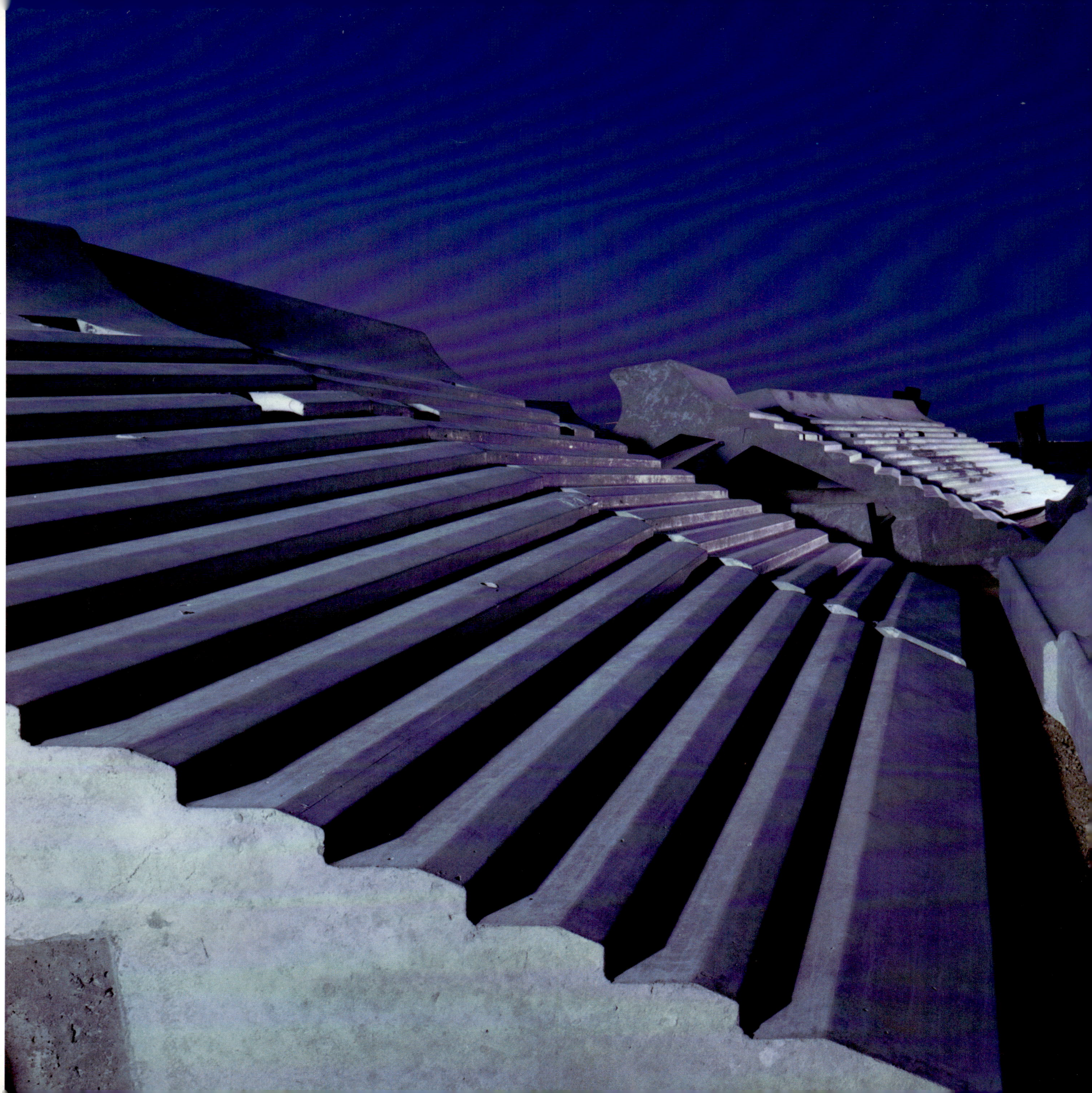

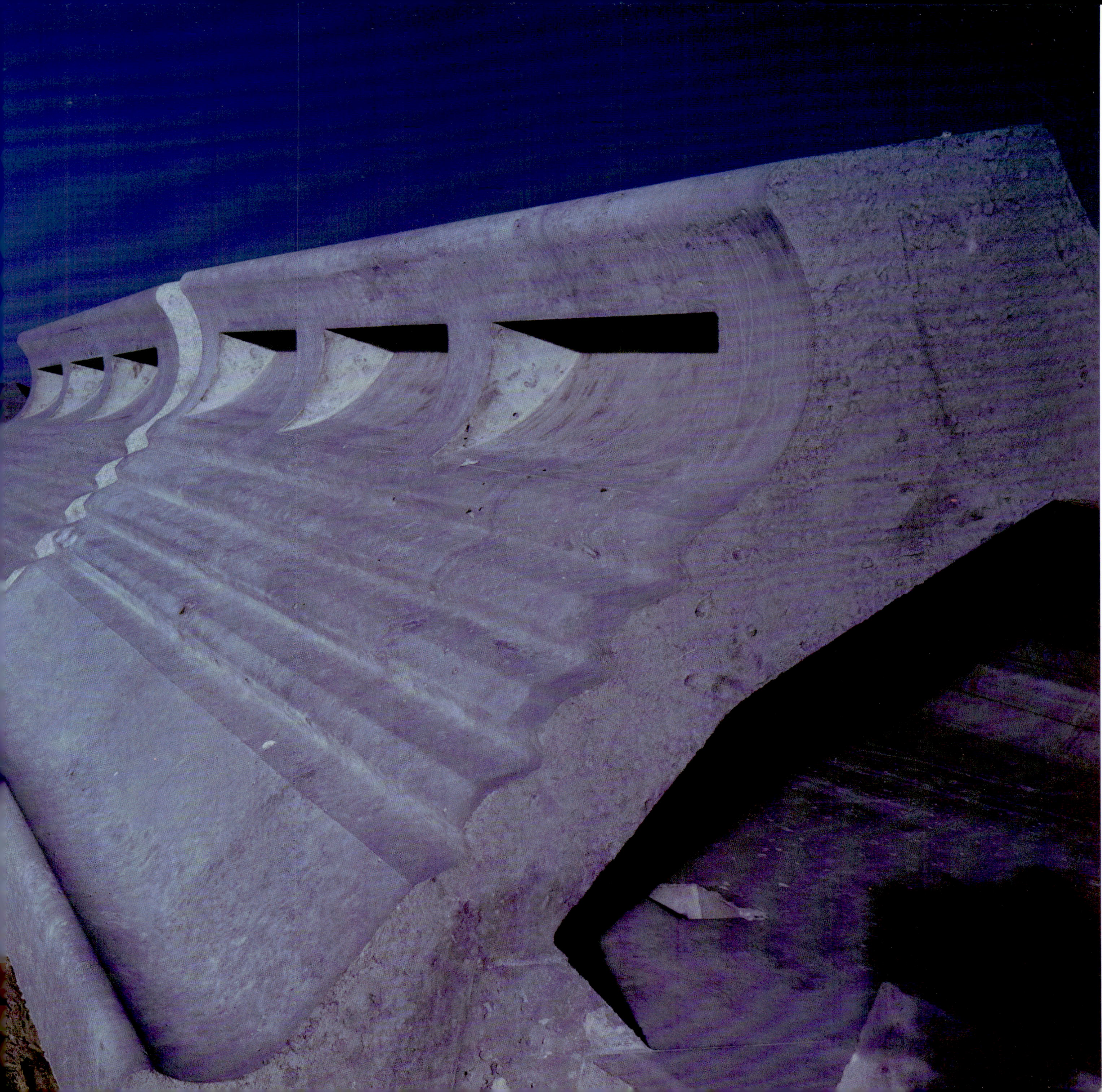

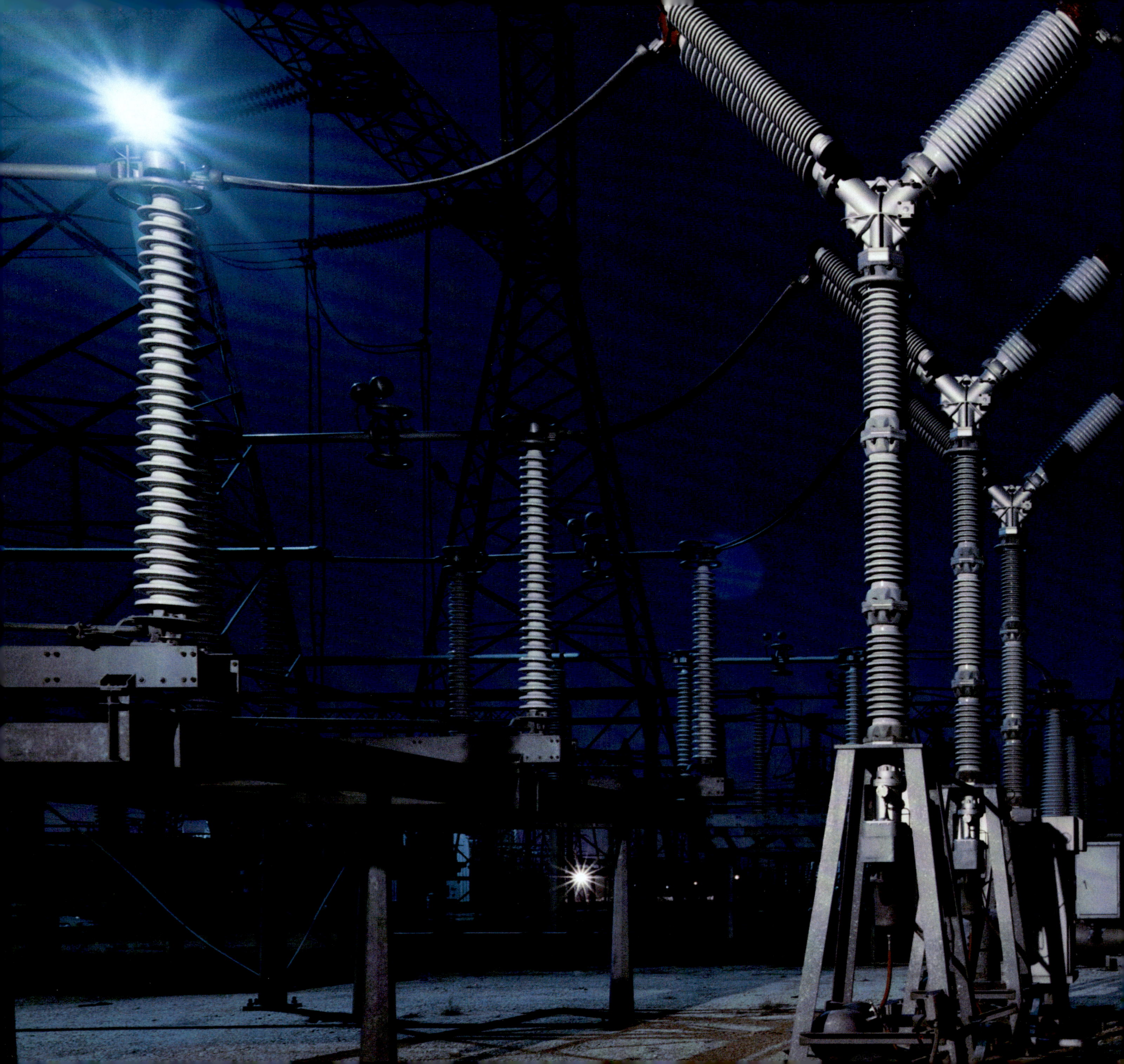

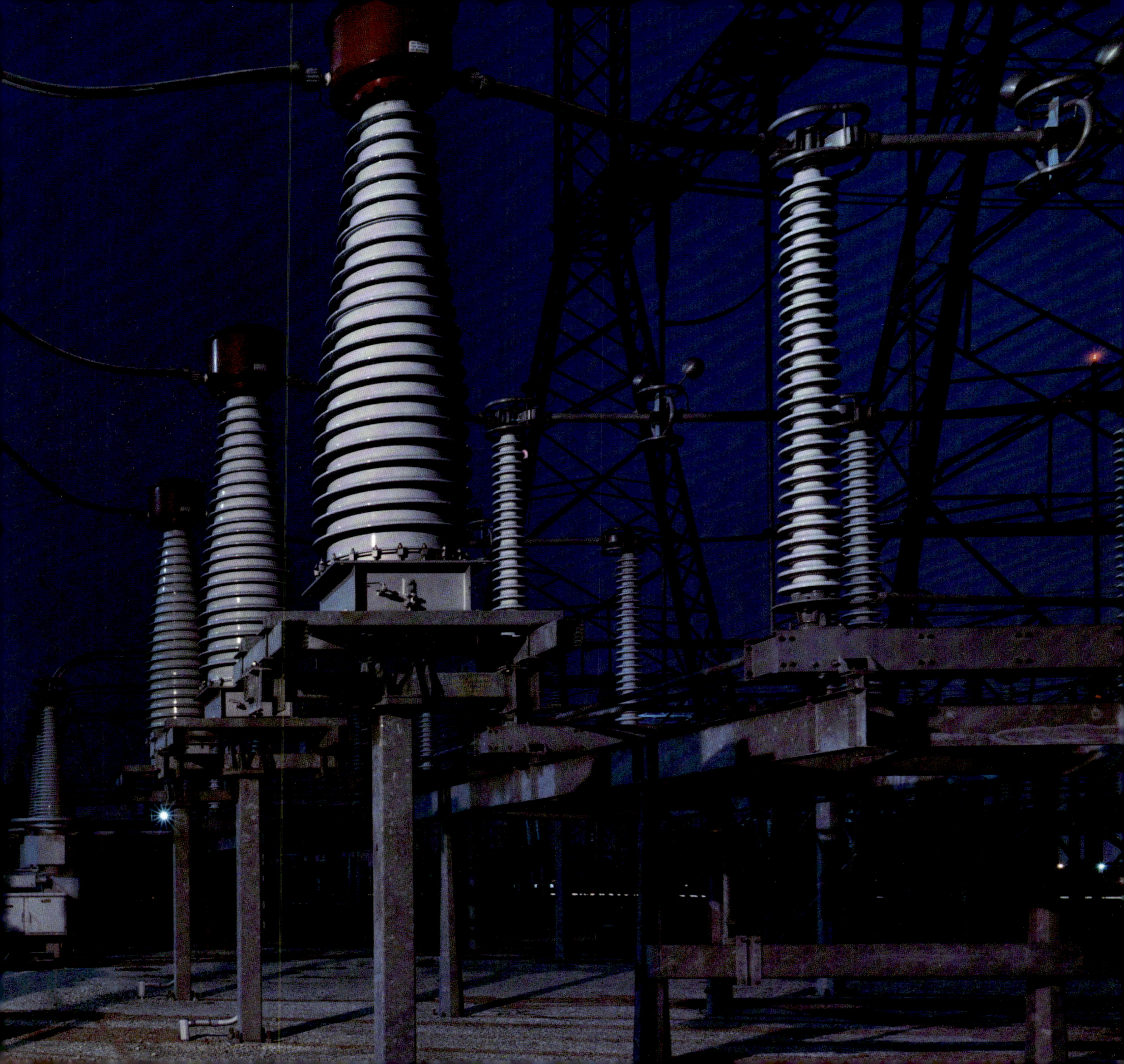

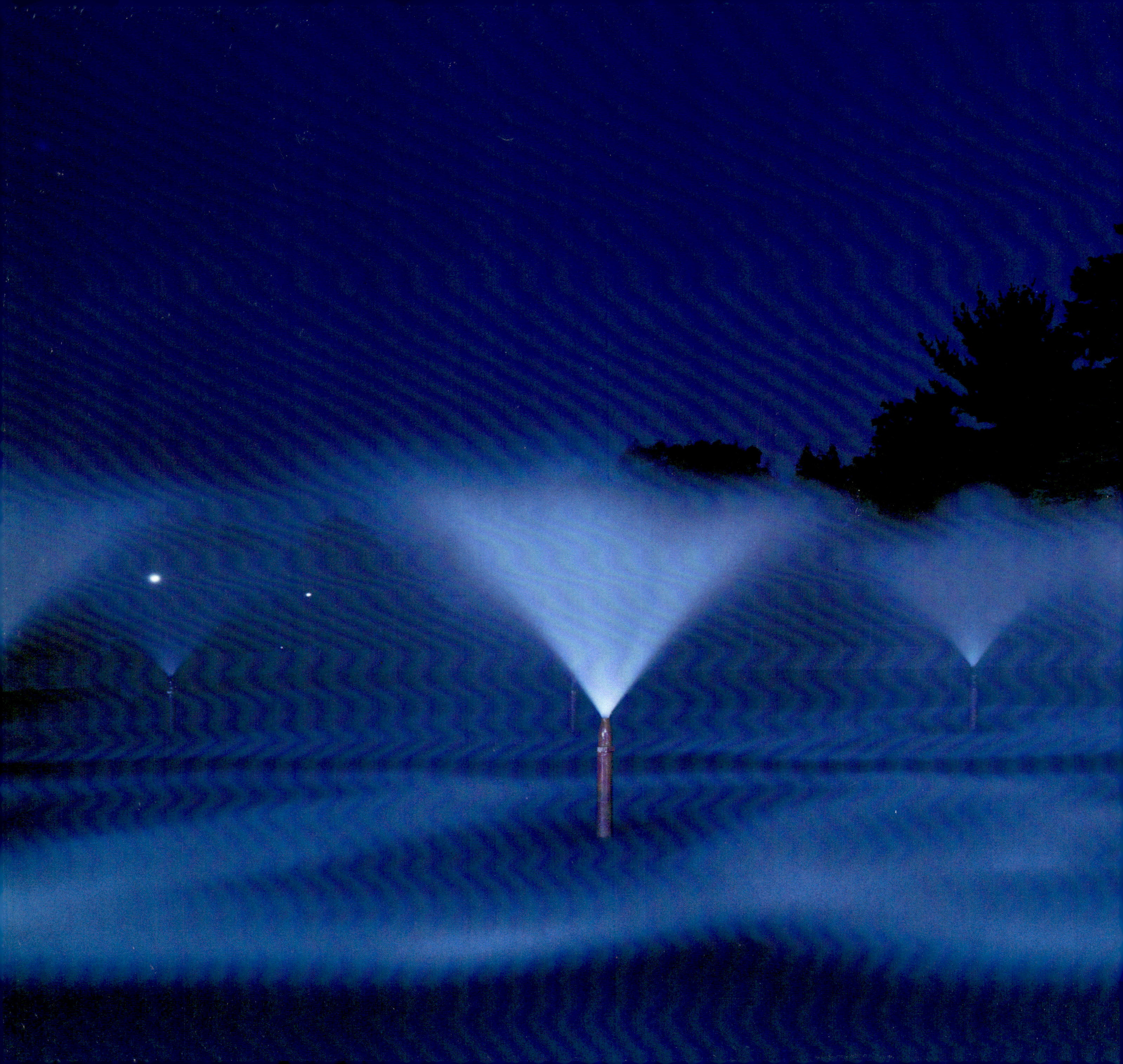

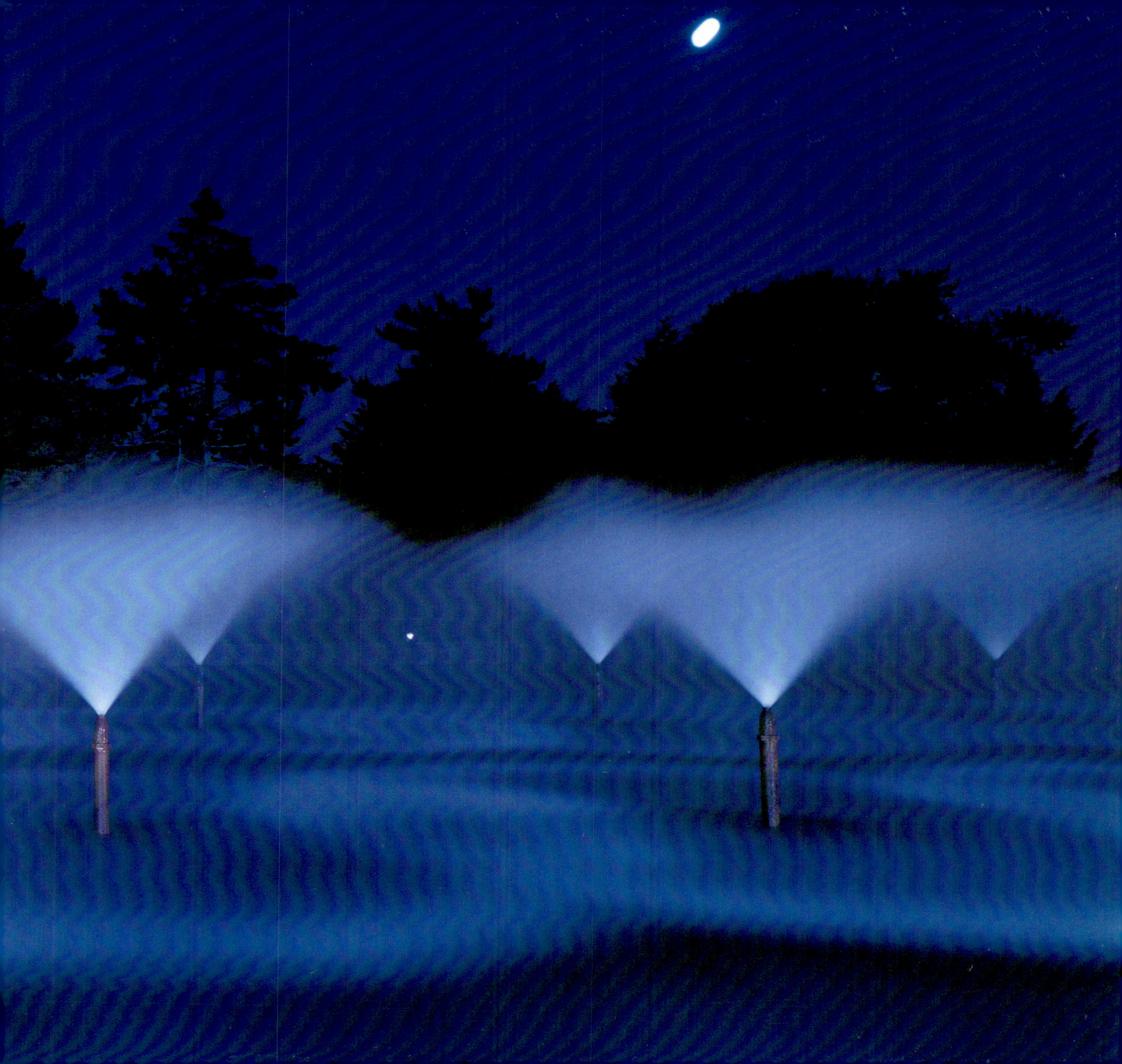

# KEY TO THE PHOTOGRAPHS

**2-3** Electromagnetic pulse testing facility, nuclear weapons laboratory at Kirtland Air Force Base, Albuquerque, New Mexico. Scientific research device using a gigantic, horizontally configured Jacob's Ladder apparatus. Full-size airplanes can be located between parallel wire grids, and an electric charge passes through the test subject to simulate the electrical pulse of a nuclear explosion. I was intrigued with the wire gridding of the landscape, which I found suggestive of the grids used for perspective in landscape painting.

**4-5** Sedan crater, Nevada Test Site. The Atomic Energy Commission, in their 1960s program "Atoms for Peace," were looking for ways to create a more positive public attitude toward nuclear explosions, so they resourcefully experimented by using bombs for civilian applications, such as the making of large holes in the ground.

**6-7** Corrugated steel pipe used for cattle drinking water.

**15** Earth augers, Midland, Michigan. Used for drilling holes in the earth so that cardboard tube forms can be inserted in the ground. Once placed in the holes, the tubes are filled with concrete.

**16** Rocks on black felt. Construction site alongside new highway and likely built for flood control.

**17** Metal Plates. These plates are being used as tree anchors for landscaping on the roof of a New York City sewage treatment center.

**18** Bricks on pilings.

**19** Tarpaper cones. These were fabricated by me in an effort to photographically realize a vision that I had had when I visited a construction site in New Jersey. I attempted to photograph a similar array of tarpaper cones placed in small holes in the earth, but was unsuccessful because the black tarpaper was indiscernible on the film. I then made my own cones of tarpaper painted silver on one side, and this is the resulting image.

**20** Alamagordo, New Mexico.

**21** Moon and stars, Dubois, Wyoming. Seven-hour photograph of faint light patches spilling onto the landscape from a nearby cabin. The traces of the moon and stars can be seen traveling across the sky as the night passed.

**22-23** Windmills, Mojave, California. Twenty-second exposure.

**24** Window frame, Nevada Test Site. Part of an array of typical construction techniques placed on the desert where atmospheric bomb tests were conducted. Various structures were used to test the effects of nuclear bomb explosions on building materials and methods.

**25** Concrete pilings.

**27** Trinity Site, New Mexico. The site of the first atomic bomb test is marked with an obelisk. This horrendous event is commemorated by a trivial monument better suited to a suburban backyard. I had just finished photographing the monument from the opposite side when I noticed that the moon had risen behind me. When I walked around to the other side and switched on my lamp, the shadow from the light shining through a small steel guard made the odd drawing on the sand. A case of fortuitous happenstance.

**28** Sepulcher, Jersey City.

**29** Trash television. The TV set was dumped in the marshlands near Jersey City. I smashed open the back of the picture tube and illuminated the screen with an emergency roadflare from my car.

**31** "Rock of Cages." Sound abatement wall at construction site near route 287 in Summit, New Jersey.

**32** Gabions. These wire cages are used to construct rock walls similar to those seen in the previous image.

**33** Unknown object, unknown function (to me). Possibly a boiler or condenser, which I lit with artificial light.

**34-35** Landfill. Garbage trucks unloading at twilight, Brooklyn, New York.

**36** Construction site, bridge supports.

**37** Abandoned train trestle piers from a dismantled rail facility. Jersey City.

**39** Spherical fiberglass gas tank, New Jersey. While exploring New Jersey, I noticed hundreds of these balls in the storage yard of the factory. As I was there on a Sunday, and the compound was not fenced off, I was able to roll one of the balls off to the side. I used the two metal halide parking field lamps that I carry in the car to illuminate the ball from front and behind.

**40** Channel Tunnel, Sangatte, France.

**41** Tripod with tires, Port Reading, New Jersey. This construction, which to me suggests a lost Rauschenberg assemblage, appears to be both a marker and protection for the plastic pipe within the tripod's legs. I assume that the pipe is a groundwater sampling well.

**42** Police department gun range, Jersey City.

**43** Spiral staircase, Williamsburg Bridge, Brooklyn, New York.

**44-45** Frenchman Flats, Nevada Test Site. Prototype for bomb-blast-survivable bunker construction, built in the sixties during the atmospheric bomb testing program.

**46** Sewage treatment plant, before the proverbial "shit hits the fan." First test running of facility, Brooklyn, New York.

**47** Ground Zero, New York City.

**48** Rooftop of a natural gas storage facility, Brooklyn, New York.

**49** Gasometer, Elmhurst, New York.

**50** Exploded oil tank, Wyoming.

**51** Ruined golf driving range, New York City.

**52-53** Nuclear weapons laboratory, Kirtland Airforce Base, Albuquerque, New Mexico.

**54-55** Frenchman Flats, Nevada Test Site. Prototype for bomb-blast-survivable bunker construction built in the sixties during the atmospheric bomb testing program.

**56** Nuclear weapons laboratory, Kirtland Airforce Base, Albuquerque, New Mexico.

**57** Field, Carlsbad, New Mexico.

**58-59** Mayan pyramid, Port Reading, New Jersey.

**60** Gravel pile. Dam construction site, Warnaque Resevoir, New Jersey.

**61** Cancelled construction site, nuclear power plant.

**62** Moonrise over Martinez, Wyoming.

**63** Salt mountain, Perth Amboy, New Jersey.

**64** Farmer's silage, Germany.

**65** Tapioca storage, Portland Maine. I have long been fascinated with the otherwordly look of the vinyl airstructures. This was one that I had attempted to photograph from the outside, but found no inspiration once I began photographing it. Out of curiosity, I decided to look inside the structure and subsequently made this image.

**66** Jones Beach parking lot.

**67** Horton waterspheroid, Point Lookout, Long Island. This location and the image opposite are from the area where I spent the first ten years of my life, and later returned to photograph.

**68** Ghost car, Jersey City.

**69** Sand blaster.

**70-71** Launch bunker, Cape Canaveral.

**72** Dormant steel mill, Buffalo, New York.

**73** Pipe configuration, uranium processing facility.

**74** Ruins of Roebling steel mill.

**75** Workshop, ruins of state penitentiary, Philadelphia, Pennsylvania.

**76** Cancelled nuclear reactor, Hartsville, Tennessee.

**77** Electrical substation, Houston, Texas.

**78** Greenhouse, Thailand.

**79** Tapioca plants, Thailand.

**80** Cows, Thailand.

**81** Cows, Louisiana.

**82** Concrete pilings, Hudson River, New York City.

**83** Cast concrete sewage junction boxes.

**84** Gas pipeline, water-depth rule, discarded tire, Port Elizabeth, New Jersey. My assumption here is that this is an offshore gas line which would have been floated out into the harbor by using the plastic barrels for buoyancy. The barrels would then be cut off to allow the pipeline to sink.

**85** Unfinished sewage treatment plant, Tampa, Florida.

**86-87** Rocket telemetry equipment, White Sands Missile Range, New Mexico.

**88-89** Electrical substation.

**90-91** Water purification plant, Hempstead, Long Island.

# AFTERWORD

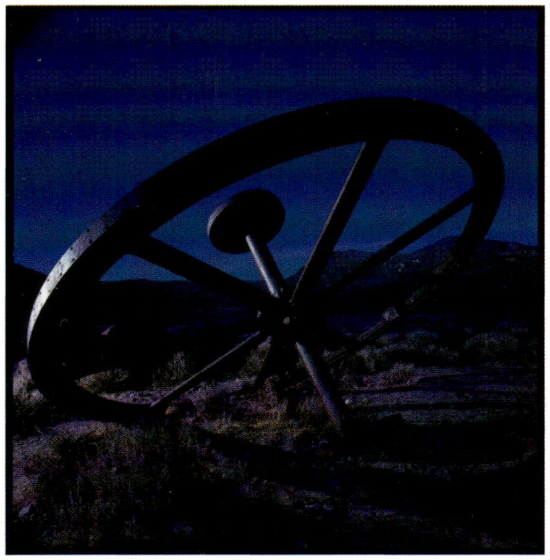

The photographic image that I create is not a faithful description of the site at which it was made. The subject matter is often markedly transformed by my imagery through the use of lighting, color, framing, and scale.

For the work in this volume—made over a period of fifteen years—I have photographed happenstance arrangements of various materials found at construction and industrial sites. Defense and nuclear facilities have also been a source for my work. Common to all of my imagery is a landscape altered by some element of human activity. Rather than directly address the pedagogical issues of nature laid to waste, as documentary photographs do, my photographs attempt to imbue the site with an edge of mystery and foreboding. Departing from the traditions of earthworks and minimalism, I look for the power and beauty of monumental sculpture that can sometimes be found in objects meant to perform some workaday function.

The surreal hues in my images result from the film's response to the light sources found in many of the locations in which I work. The combination of twilight and industrial lighting causes color distortions to the illuminated objects. Adjusting for these inaccuracies when I make the print can alter the color of the sky, producing an otherworldly atmosphere. With one or two exceptions, I have not altered the scenes in my pictures, except to introduce lighting. Much in the tradition of the *objet trouvé*, I encapsulate a sculptural awareness by committing my subject to film.

***—Jan Staller***

JACKET DESIGN BY Carol Devine Carson

BOOK DESIGN BY Wendy Setzer

PRINTED AND BOUND BY Mariogros Industrie Grafiche, Torino, Italy

COLOR SEPARATIONS BY Sele Offset Torino S. R. L., Italy

THE STAFF AT APERTURE FOR *ON PLANET EARTH* IS:

| | |
|---|---|
| EXECUTIVE DIRECTOR | Michael E. Hoffman |
| EDITOR | Michael Sand |
| PRODUCTION DIRECTOR | Stevan A. Baron |
| ASSISTANT EDITOR | Michael Lorenzini |
| PRODUCTION MANAGER | Helen Marra |
| EDITORIAL WORK-SCHOLAR | Mamie Thibodeau |
| PRODUCTION WORK-SCHOLAR | Shona Curtis |



Library of Congress Catalog Card Number: 97-70512

ISBN: 0-89381-730-9

Aperture Foundation publishes a periodical, books, and portfolios of fine photography to communicate with serious photographers and creative people everywhere. A complete catalog is available upon request. Address: 20 East 23rd Street, New York, New York 10010. Phone: (212) 598-4205. Fax: (212) 598-4015.

Aperture Foundation books are distributed internationally through:

**Canada**: General Publishing, 30 Lesmill Road, Don Mills, Ontario, M3B 2T6. Fax: (416) 445-5991. **United Kingdom**: Robert Hale, Ltd., Clerkenwell House, 45-47 Clerkenwell Green, London EC1R OHT. Fax: 171-490-4958. **Continental Europe**: Nilsson & Lamm, BV, Pampuslaan 212-214, P.O. Box 195, 1382 JS Weesp, Netherlands. Fax: 31-294-415054.

For international magazine subscription orders for the periodical *Aperture*, contact Aperture International Subscription Service, P.O. Box 14, Harold Hill, Romford, RM3 8EQ, England. Fax: 1-708-372-046. One year: £30.00. Price subject to change.

To subscribe to the periodical *Aperture* in the U.S.A. write Aperture, P.O. Box 3000, Denville, NJ 07834. Tel: 1-800-783-4903. One year: $40.00.

First edition
10 9 8 7 6 5 4 3 2 1

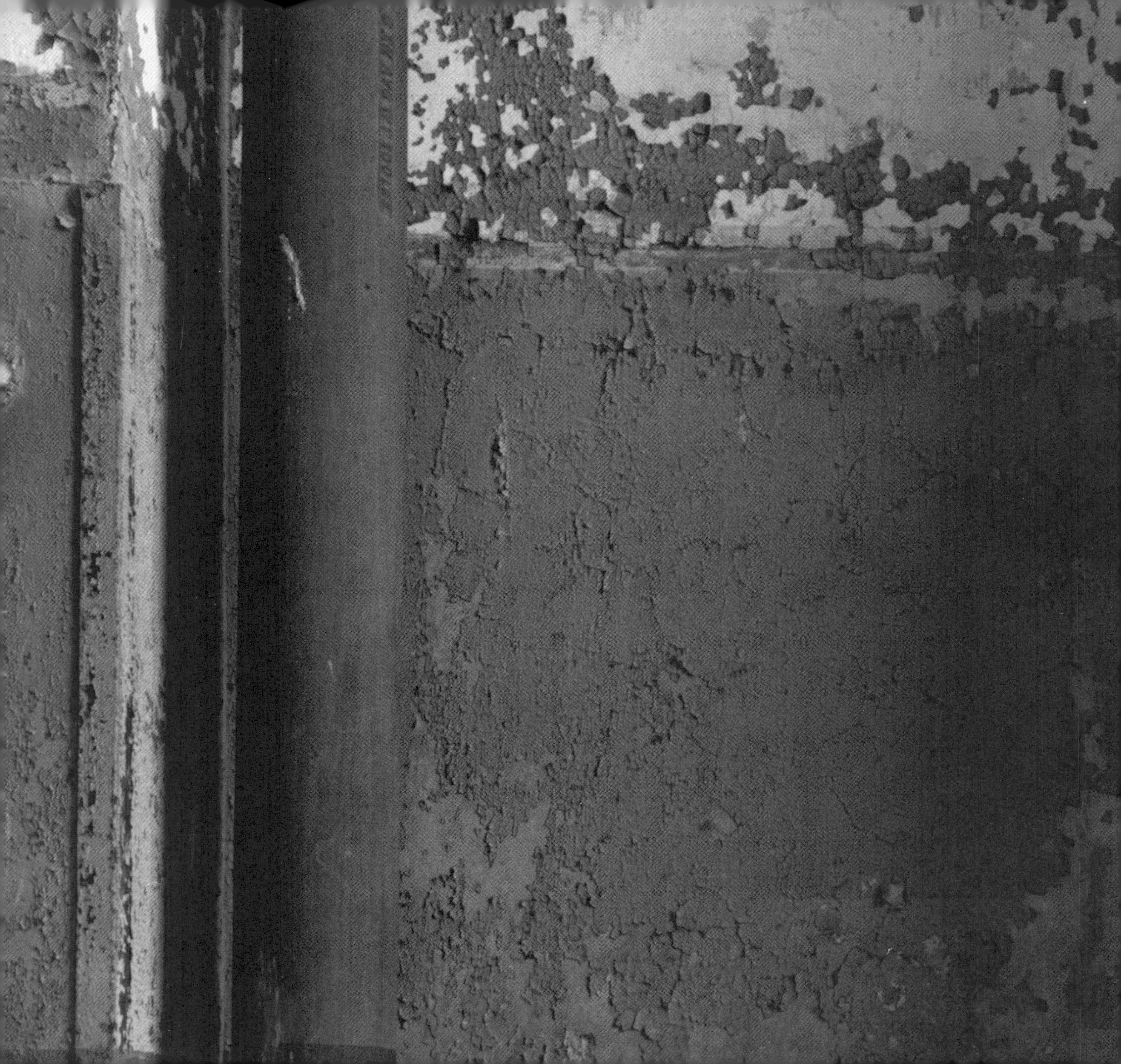